# BEST OF COUNTRY
# Brownies
## and Bars

# Best of Country Brownies and Bars

You simply can't beat a brownie. There's something about biting into those rich, handheld squares that keeps folks of all ages coming back for more…and more!

Big on finger-licking satisfaction and low on effort, scrumptious brownies and one-batch bars are all-time favorites with family bakers. That's why we compiled a mouth-watering assortment of specialties shared by cooks across the country.

Featuring 218 sweet successes, *Best of Country Brownies and Bars* offers enough recipes to meet any of your needs. Whether you're looking for a classroom treat, a contribution to a potluck or an after-supper surprise, this yummy collection has you covered! You'll even find brownie-based sensations impressive enough for weekend dinner parties.

We got things started by grouping the best-of-the-best into the chapter "Prize-Winning Delights" (p. 4). Having earned an award in one of *Taste of Home's* recipe contests, each of the treats is sure to become a new staple at your house.

Since you can't mention brownies without thinking of chocolate, we devoted a whole chapter to our fudgy favorites. See "Chocolate Sensations" on page 20 for decadent specialties, such as Double Chocolate Bars (p. 31), Chocolate Bliss Brownies (p. 33) and many more.

Looking for a change-of-pace? Consider the goodies in "Fruit-Filled Snacks" (p. 34). Blueberry Oat Bars (p. 40), Banana-Berry Brownie Pizza (p. 42) and Cherry Streusel Squares (p. 48) are some of the treats you'll find.

Some like brownies loaded with nuts, others enjoy bars layered with caramel and many reach for sweets topped with icing. Regardless of your preference, you'll find perfect tooth-tinglers in the sections "Caramel, Nuts & More" (p. 52) and "Frosted Brownies" (p. 68).

See "Time-Saving Treats" (p. 82) when you need something sweet in a flash. These brownies and bars come together in a pinch, dress up convenient mixes or have short baking times. And when you need something a bit more special, consider items such as Triple Layer Brownie Cake (p. 95), Mocha Mousse Brownie Trifle (p. 99) and Brownie Baked Alaska (p. 103). You'll find these after-dinner delicacies and others in the chapter "Brownie Desserts" which begins on page 94.

Whichever recipes you try, you're sure to find winners with your family. Bake up a batch today, and see just how easy it is to brighten someone's day with brownies and bars that are truly the best in the country.

**Senior Editor/Books:** Mark Hagen
**Art Director:** Gretchen Trautman
**Vice President, Executive Editor/Books:** Heidi Reuter Lloyd
**Layout Designer:** Emma Acevedo
**Proofreader:** Linne Bruskewitz
**Associate Editors:** Sara Lancaster, Jean Steiner
**Editorial Assistant:** Barb Czysz
**Food Director:** Diane Werner RD
**Test Kitchen Manager:** Karen Scales
**Recipe Editors:** Sue A. Jurack (Senior), Mary King, Christine Rukavena
**Recipe Asset System Manager:** Coleen Martin

**Studio Photographers:** Rob Hagen (Senior), Dan Roberts, Jim Wieland, Lori Foy
**Senior Food Stylists:** Sarah Thompson, Joylyn Trickel
**Food Stylist Assistants:** Kaitlyn Basasie, Alynna Malson
**Set Stylists:** Jennifer Bradley Vent (Senior), Dee Dee Schaefer
**Photo Studio Coordinator:** Kathleen Swaney
**Creative Director:** Ardyth Cope

**Senior Vice President, Editor in Chief:** Catherine Cassidy

©2007 Reiman Media Group, LLC
5400 S. 60th St., Greendale WI 53129
International Standard Book Number (10): 0-89821-549-8
International Standard Book Number (13): 978-089821-549-6
Library of Congress Control Number: 2007928050

**Pictured on the front cover:** Double Frosted Brownies (p. 76), Peanut Butter Brownies (p. 62), Chippy Blond Brownies (p. 60) and Caramel Brownies (p. 64). **Pictured on title page:** Double Frosted Brownies (p. 76), Rustic Nut Bars (p. 60), Raspberry Nut Bars (p. 36), Peanut Butter Brownies (p. 62) and Chippy Blond Brownies (p. 60). **Pictured on back cover:** Golden M&M Bars (p. 62), Frosted Cookie Brownies (p. 77), Blueberry Lattice Bars (p. 43) and Raspberry Almond Bars (p. 7).

# BEST OF COUNTRY

# Brownies and Bars

# Chapter 1

p. 11

p. 7

p. 9

p. 18

p. 19

# Prize-Winning Delights

These gobble-me-up goodies take the prize every time. That's because the rich morsels are among the best-of-the-best from the *Taste of Home* baking contests.

In a small mixing bowl, beat cream cheese until smooth. Beat in confectioners' sugar, melted chocolate and coffee. Spread over brownies.

For glaze, melt the chocolate chips and shortening in a heavy saucepan or microwave; stir until smooth. Drizzle over filling. Refrigerate for at least 2 hours before cutting. Store in the refrigerator. **Yield:** about 6-1/2 dozen.

## Butter Fudge Fingers

Peggy Mangus, Worland, Wyoming

These scrumptious brownies get dressed up with a delicious browned butter frosting. The combination is delightfully different and assures that these yummy treats vanish fast around the house or at a party.

  2/3  cup butter, cubed
    4  squares (1 ounce *each*) unsweetened chocolate
    4  eggs
    1  teaspoon salt
    2  cups sugar
1-1/2  cups all-purpose flour
    1  teaspoon baking powder
    1  cup chopped pecans
BROWNED BUTTER FROSTING:
  1/2  cup butter, cubed
    4  cups confectioners' sugar
  1/3  cup heavy whipping cream
    2  teaspoons vanilla extract
GLAZE:
    1  square (1 ounce) unsweetened chocolate
    1  tablespoon butter

In a microwave or double boiler, melt butter and chocolate; cool for 10 minutes.

In a large mixing bowl, beat eggs and salt until foamy. Gradually add sugar until well blended. Stir in chocolate

mocha truffle brownies

## Mocha Truffle Brownies

Margaret Roberts, Kuna, Idaho

My husband is a chocolate lover, so I bake brownies about once a week. This mouth-watering variety is one of his all-time favorites. They're so simple to make, too.

1-1/4  cups semisweet chocolate chips
  1/2  cup butter
    1  teaspoon instant coffee granules
    2  tablespoons hot water
    2  eggs
  3/4  cup packed brown sugar
  3/4  cup all-purpose flour
  1/2  teaspoon baking powder
FILLING:
    1  tablespoon instant coffee granules
    1  tablespoon hot water
    1  package (8 ounces) cream cheese, softened
  1/3  cup confectioners' sugar
    1  cup (6 ounces) semisweet chocolate chips, melted
GLAZE:
  1/4  cup semisweet chocolate chips
    1  teaspoon shortening

In a heavy saucepan or microwave, melt chips and butter. Stir until smooth; cool for 5 minutes. Dissolve coffee granules in hot water; set aside. In a large mixing bowl, beat eggs and brown sugar; beat on medium for 1 minute. Stir in chocolate mixture and coffee. Combine flour and baking powder; gradually add to chocolate mixture.

Transfer to a greased 9-in. square baking pan. Bake at 350° for 30-35 minutes or until a toothpick inserted near the center comes out with moist crumbs. Cool completely on a wire rack.

For filling, dissolve coffee granules in water; set aside.

butter fudge fingers

raspberry almond bars

mixture. Combine flour and baking powder; gradually add to batter. Stir in pecans.

Pour into a greased 15-in. x 10-in. x 1-in. baking pan. Bake at 350° for 20-25 minutes or until a toothpick inserted near the center comes out clean. Cool in pan on a wire rack.

For frosting, in a large heavy saucepan, cook butter over medium heat for 5-7 minutes or until golden brown. Pour into a large mixing bowl; beat in the confectioners' sugar, cream and vanilla until smooth. Frost bars.

For glaze, in a microwave, melt the chocolate and butter; stir until smooth. Cool slightly. Drizzle over bars. **Yield:** about 5 dozen.

## Raspberry Almond Bars

Mimi Priesman, Pace, Florida

A co-worker's mother gave me a gem of a recipe a few years back. I can never decide what's more appealing—the attractive look of the bars or their incredible aroma while they're baking!

|     |                                                       |
| --- | ----------------------------------------------------- |
| 1/2 | cup butter, cubed                                     |
| 1   | package (10 to 12 ounces) vanilla *or* white chips, *divided* |
| 2   | eggs                                                  |
| 1/2 | cup sugar                                             |
| 1   | teaspoon almond extract                               |
| 1   | cup all-purpose flour                                 |
| 1/2 | teaspoon salt                                         |
| 1/2 | cup seedless raspberry jam                            |
| 1/4 | cup sliced almonds                                    |

In a small saucepan, melt butter. Remove from the heat; add 1 cup chips (do not stir). In a small mixing bowl, beat eggs until foamy; gradually add sugar. Stir in chip mixture and almond extract. Combine flour and salt; add to egg mixture just until combined.

Spread half of the batter into a greased 9-in. square baking pan. Bake at 325° for 15-20 minutes or until golden brown.

In a small saucepan, melt jam over low heat; spread over warm crust. Stir remaining chips into the remaining batter; drop by teaspoonfuls over the jam layer. Sprinkle with almonds.

Bake 30-35 minutes longer or until a toothpick inserted near the center comes out clean. Cool on a wire rack. Cut into bars. **Yield:** 2 dozen.

## Snow Flurry Brownies

Sherry Olson, Boulder, Colorado

These brownies are the best dessert in my recipe box. I've even prepared them on the spur of the moment while company was over for dinner. They take just minutes to mix up, are out of the oven in half an hour and result in lots of compliments.

|     |                                    |
| --- | ---------------------------------- |
| 1   | cup sugar                          |
| 1/2 | cup butter, melted                 |
| 2   | eggs                               |
| 1/2 | teaspoon vanilla extract           |
| 2/3 | cup all-purpose flour              |
| 1/2 | cup baking cocoa                   |
| 1/2 | teaspoon baking powder             |
| 1/2 | teaspoon salt                      |
| 1/2 | cup vanilla *or* white chips       |
| 1/2 | cup chopped macadamia nuts *or* almonds |

In a large bowl, whisk together the sugar, butter, eggs and vanilla. Combine the flour, cocoa, baking powder and salt; add to sugar mixture until well blended. Stir in vanilla chips and nuts.

Spread into a greased 8-in. square baking pan. Bake at 350° for 25-30 minutes or until a toothpick inserted near the center comes out with moist crumbs (do not overbake). Cool on a wire rack. Cut into diamond shapes if desired. **Yield:** 16 brownies.

snow flurry brownies

## Cream Cheese Swirl Brownies

Heidi Johnson, Worland, Wyoming

I'm a chocolate lover, and this treat has satisfied my cravings many times. No one guesses the brownies are lighter than others because their chewy texture and chocolate flavor can't be beat. My family requests them often, and I'm happy to oblige.

- 3 eggs
- 6 tablespoons reduced-fat stick-margarine
- 1 cup sugar, *divided*
- 3 teaspoons vanilla extract
- 1/2 cup all-purpose flour
- 1/4 cup baking cocoa
- 1 package (8 ounces) reduced-fat cream cheese

Separate two eggs, putting each white in a separate bowl (discard yolks or save for another use); set aside. In a small mixing bowl, beat margarine and 3/4 cup sugar until crumbly. Add the whole egg, one egg white and vanilla; mix well. Combine flour and cocoa; add to egg mixture and beat until blended. Pour into a 9-in. square baking pan coated with nonstick cooking spray; set aside.

In a mixing bowl, beat cream cheese and remaining sugar until smooth. Beat in the second egg white. Drop by rounded tablespoonfuls over the batter; cut through batter with a knife to swirl. Bake at 350° for 25-30 minutes or until set and edges pull away from sides of pan. Cool on a wire rack. **Yield:** 1 dozen.

*Editor's Note:* *This recipe was tested with Parkay Light stick margarine.*

cream cheese swirl brownies

out-of-this-world brownies

## Out-of-This-World Brownies

Jeannette Haley, Council, Idaho

Every time I host company or attend a bake sale, I whip up a batch of these fabulous brownies. Most everyone who tastes them says, "Yum! These are the best brownies I have ever eaten!"

- 1 cup butter, softened
- 2 cups sugar
- 4 eggs
- 2 teaspoons vanilla extract
- 2 cups all-purpose flour
- 1/4 cup plus 3 tablespoons baking cocoa
- 1/8 teaspoon salt
BROWNED BUTTER FROSTING:
- 1/2 cup butter
- 4 cups confectioners' sugar
- 1/4 cup plus 2 teaspoons half-and-half cream
- 2 teaspoons vanilla extract
GLAZE:
- 1 square (1 ounce) unsweetened chocolate
- 1 tablespoon butter

In a large mixing bowl, cream butter and sugar until light and fluffy. Add eggs, one at a time, beating well after each addition. Beat in vanilla. Combine flour, cocoa and salt; gradually add to the creamed mixture.

Spread into an ungreased 13-in. x 9-in. x 2-in. baking pan. Bake at 350° for 25-30 minutes or until a toothpick inserted near the center comes out clean (do not overbake). Cool on wire rack.

For frosting, in a heavy saucepan, cook and stir butter over medium heat for 5-7 minutes or until golden brown. Pour into a mixing bowl; beat in the confectioners' sugar, cream and vanilla. Frost cooled brownies.

For glaze, in a microwave melt chocolate and butter; stir until smooth. Drizzle over the frosting. Cut into bars. **Yield:** 3 dozen.

fudgy mint squares

## Two-Tone Fudge Brownies

Rebecca Kays, Klamath Falls, Oregon

These moist, fudgy brownies have a scrumptious topping that tastes just like chocolate chip cookie dough! Everyone loves these brownies...and they make enough to share with lots of friends.

- 1 cup (6 ounces) semisweet chocolate chips
- 1/2 cup butter, softened
- 1 cup sugar
- 3 eggs
- 1 teaspoon vanilla extract
- 1-1/4 cups all-purpose flour
- 1/4 teaspoon baking soda
- 3/4 cup chopped walnuts

COOKIE DOUGH LAYER:
- 1/2 cup butter, softened
- 1/2 cup packed brown sugar
- 1/4 cup sugar
- 3 tablespoons milk
- 1 teaspoon vanilla extract
- 1 cup all-purpose flour
- 1 cup (6 ounces) semisweet chocolate chips

In a microwave, melt chocolate chips; stir until smooth. Cool slightly. In a large mixing bowl, cream butter and sugar until smooth. Beat in eggs and vanilla. Stir in melted chocolate. Combine flour and baking soda; gradually add to batter. Stir in walnuts.

Spread into a greased 13-in. x 9-in. x 2-in. baking pan. Bake at 350° for 16-22 minutes or until a toothpick inserted near the center comes out clean. Cool brownies on a wire rack.

In a small mixing bowl, cream butter and sugars until light and fluffy. Beat in milk and vanilla. Gradually add flour. Stir in chocolate chips. Drop by tablespoonfuls over cooled brownies; carefully spread over top. Cut into squares. Store in the refrigerator. **Yield:** 4 dozen.

two-tone fudge brownies

## Fudgy Mint Squares

Heather Campbell, Lawrence, Kansas

I've had this recipe since I was in junior high school. No one can resist the fudgy brownie base, cool minty cheesecake filling and luscious chocolate glaze in these mouthwatering bars.

- 10 tablespoons butter, *divided*
- 3 squares (1 ounce *each*) unsweetened chocolate, chopped
- 3 eggs
- 1-1/2 cups sugar
- 2 teaspoons vanilla extract
- 1 cup all-purpose flour
- 1 package (8 ounces) cream cheese, softened
- 1 tablespoon cornstarch
- 1 can (14 ounces) sweetened condensed milk
- 1 teaspoon peppermint extract
- 4 drops green food coloring, optional
- 1 cup (6 ounces) semisweet chocolate chips
- 1/2 cup heavy whipping cream

In a microwave, melt 8 tablespoons butter and unsweetened chocolate; stir until smooth. Cool slightly. In a small mixing bowl, beat 2 eggs, sugar and vanilla. Beat in chocolate mixture until blended. Gradually add in flour.

Spread into a greased 13-in. x 9-in. x 2-in. baking pan. Bake at 350° for 15-20 minutes or until top is set.

In a large mixing bowl, beat cream cheese and remaining butter until smooth. Add cornstarch; beat until smooth. Gradually beat in milk and remaining egg. Beat in extract and food coloring if desired.

Pour over crust. Bake for 15-20 minutes or until center is almost set. Cool on a wire rack.

In a small heavy saucepan, combine chocolate chips and cream. Cook and stir over medium heat until chips are melted. Cool for 30 minutes or until lukewarm, stirring occasionally. Pour over cream cheese layer. Chill for 2 hours or until set before cutting. **Yield**: about 4 dozen.

peanut butter squares

## Peanut Butter Squares

Rachel Keller, Roanoke, Virginia

I grew up in Lancaster County, Pennsylvania and spent a lot of time in the kitchen with my mom and grandmother making Pennsylvania Dutch classics. This scrumptious, no-bake recipe is one I created based on two of our favorite flavors.

- 3/4 cup cold butter, cubed
- 2 squares (1 ounce *each*) semisweet chocolate
- 1-1/2 cups graham cracker crumbs (about 24 squares)
- 1 cup flaked coconut
- 1/2 cup chopped salted peanuts
- 1/4 cup toasted wheat germ

FILLING:
- 2 packages (8 ounces *each*) cream cheese, softened
- 3/4 cup sugar
- 2/3 cup chunky peanut butter
- 1 teaspoon vanilla extract

TOPPING:
- 4 squares (1 ounce *each*) semisweet chocolate
- 1/4 cup butter, cubed

In a microwave-safe bowl, heat butter and chocolate on high for 45 seconds; stir. Microwave 20-50 seconds longer or until melted; stir until smooth. Stir in cracker crumbs, coconut, peanuts and wheat germ. Press into a greased 13-in. x 9-in. x 2-in. pan. Cover and refrigerate for at least 30 minutes.

In a small mixing bowl, combine filling ingredients; mix well. Spread over crust. Cover and refrigerate for at least 30 minutes.

In a microwave-safe bowl, heat the chocolate and butter on high for 35 seconds; stir. Microwave 20 seconds longer or until melted; stir until smooth. Pour over filling. Cover and refrigerate for at least 30 minutes or until topping is set. Cut into squares. Refrigerate leftovers. **Yield:** 4 dozen.

*Editor's Note: This recipe was tested in a 1,100-watt microwave.*

## Chocolate Cheese Layered Bars

Sharon Schaa, Murray, Iowa

You just can't beat these decadent, cheesecake bars. Featuring lots of chocolate flavor, the luscious bars are a standout on any dessert buffet.

- 1/2 cup butter, softened
- 1 cup sugar
- 2 eggs
- 1 square (1 ounce) unsweetened chocolate, melted
- 1 teaspoon vanilla extract
- 1 cup all-purpose flour
- 1 teaspoon baking powder
- 1/2 cup chopped pecans

CHEESE LAYER:
- 6 ounces cream cheese, softened
- 1/4 cup butter, softened
- 1/2 cup sugar
- 1 egg
- 2 tablespoons all-purpose flour
- 1/2 teaspoon vanilla extract
- 1/4 cup chopped pecans
- 1 cup (6 ounces) semisweet chocolate chips
- 3 cups miniature marshmallows

TOPPING:
- 1/4 cup butter
- 2 ounces cream cheese, softened
- 1 square (1 ounce) unsweetened chocolate
- 2 tablespoons milk
- 3 cup confectioners' sugar
- 1 teaspoon vanilla extract

In a large mixing bowl, cream butter and sugar. Add eggs, chocolate and vanilla; mix well. Combine flour and baking powder; stir into the chocolate mixture. Fold in the pecans. Pour into a greased 13-in. x 9-in. x 2-in. baking pan.

In a large mixing bowl, combine cream cheese and butter. Beat in the sugar, egg, flour and vanilla; mix

chocolate cheese layered bars

treasured brownies

well. Fold in pecans. Spread over the chocolate layer; sprinkle with chips.

Bake at 350° for 20-25 minutes or until edges pull away from sides of pan. Sprinkle with marshmallow; bake 2 minutes longer or until puffed. Spread evenly over cream cheese layer. Cool on a wire rack.

In a large saucepan, combine first four topping ingredients. Cook and stir over low heat until smooth. Transfer to a large mixing bowl. Add the confectioners' sugar and vanilla; beat until smooth. Spread over cooled bars. Store in the refrigerator. **Yield:** 2 dozen.

## Treasured Brownies

Marianne Wolfe, Westlock, Alberta

Here's a terrific treat that was included in a book of good-but-easy recipes my sister compiled as a wedding present for me. She refers to them as "money-back guarantee" brownies. And I can truly confirm that they turn out 100% of the time.

```
    1    cup butter, melted and cooled
    3    eggs
1-1/2    teaspoons vanilla extract
    1    cup all-purpose flour
    1    cup sugar
    1    cup packed brown sugar
  3/4    cup baking cocoa
1-1/2    teaspoons baking powder
    1    cup chopped nuts
ICING:
  1/2    cup butter, softened
1-1/4    cups confectioners' sugar
  2/3    cup baking cocoa
    2    tablespoons milk
    2    tablespoons hot brewed coffee
    1    teaspoon vanilla extract
```

In a large mixing bowl, beat the butter, eggs and vanilla. Combine the dry ingredients; gradually add to butter mixture. Stir in nuts (do not overmix).

Spread into a greased 13-in. x 9-in. x 2-in. baking pan. Bake at 350° for 25-30 minutes or until a toothpick inserted near the center of the brownies comes out clean. Cool on a wire rack.

In a small mixing bowl, beat the icing ingredients until smooth. Spread over cooled brownies. Cut into bars. **Yield:** 1-1/2 dozen.

## Jewel Nut Bars

Joyce Fitt, Listowel, Ontario

With the eye-catching appeal of candied cherries and the crunchy goodness of mixed nuts, these colorful bars are certain to become a holiday staple year after year.

```
1-1/4    cups all-purpose flour
  2/3    cup packed brown sugar, divided
  3/4    cup cold butter
    1    egg
  1/2    teaspoon salt
1-1/2    cups mixed nuts
1-1/2    cups green and red candied cherries, halved
    1    cup (6 ounces) semisweet chocolate chips
```

In a bowl, combine flour and 1/3 cup brown sugar; cut in butter until mixture resembles coarse crumbs. Press into a lightly greased 13-in. x 9-in. x 2-in. baking pan. Bake at 350° for 15 minutes.

In a large mixing bowl, beat egg. Add salt and remaining brown sugar. Stir in the nuts, cherries and chocolate chips. Spoon evenly over crust. Bake 20-25 minutes longer or until set. Cool on a wire rack. Cut into bars. **Yield:** 3 dozen.

jewel nut bars

macaroon brownies

## Macaroon Brownies

### Christine Foust, Stoneboro, Pennsylvania

My mother-in-law made these coconut-filled brownies for my bridal shower and wedding reception. After the first bite, I knew why my husband loved them!

    1    cup butter, softened
    2    cups sugar
    4    eggs
    1    teaspoon vanilla extract
    2    cups all-purpose flour
    1/2  cup baking cocoa
    1/2  teaspoon cream of tartar
    1/2  cup chopped walnuts
MACAROON FILLING:
    1    package (14 ounces) flaked coconut
    1    can (14 ounces) sweetened condensed milk
    2    teaspoons vanilla extract
FROSTING:
    3/4  cup sugar
    1/4  cup milk
    2    tablespoons butter
    1    cup miniature marshmallows
    1    cup (6 ounces) semisweet chocolate chips
    1    teaspoon vanilla extract

In a large mixing bowl, cream butter and sugar until light and fluffy. Add eggs and vanilla; mix well. Combine the flour, cocoa and cream of tartar; gradually add to creamed mixture. Stir in nuts. Spread half into a greased 13-in. x 9-in. x 2-in. baking pan.

For filling, combine the coconut, condensed milk and vanilla; carefully spread over batter in pan. Top with the remaining batter. Bake at 350° for 40-45 minutes or until a toothpick inserted near the center comes out clean. Cool on a wire rack.

For frosting, combine the sugar, milk and butter in a saucepan; cook and stir until sugar is dissolved. Add the marshmallows and chocolate chips; cook and stir until melted. Remove from the heat; stir in vanilla. Cool until frosting reaches spreading consistency, about 25 minutes. Spread over the cooled brownies. Cut into bars. **Yield:** 4 dozen.

## Caramel-Chocolate Oat Squares

### Kellie Ochsner, Newton, Iowa

In the summer, we often have weekend guests who go boating with us. These sweet, chewy bars are the perfect treat to take along. I use my microwave to prepare them, and I don't heat up the kitchen.

    3/4  cup butter, cubed
    1-1/4 cups all-purpose flour
    1-1/4 cups quick-cooking oats
    3/4  cup packed brown sugar
    1/2  teaspoon baking soda
    1/4  teaspoon salt
    24   caramels
    1/4  cup milk
    1    cup (6 ounces) semisweet chocolate chips
    1/2  cup chopped walnuts, optional

In a microwave-safe bowl, heat butter, uncovered, on high for 20-30 seconds or until softened. Combine flour, oats, brown sugar, baking soda and salt; stir into butter until blended.

Set a third of the mixture aside for topping. Press remaining mixture onto the bottom of an 8-in. square microwave-safe dish. Cook, uncovered, on high for 1-2 minutes or until crust is raised and set (crust will be uneven), rotating a half turn after each minute.

In a 1-qt. microwave-safe dish, heat the caramels and milk, uncovered, on high for 1 minute or until melted and smooth, stirring every minute. Sprinkle chips and nuts, if desired, over crust. Pour caramel mixture over all.

Sprinkle with reserved oat mixture; press down lightly. Microwave, uncovered, on high for 2-3 minutes or until the caramel is bubbly, rotating a quarter turn every minute. Cool before cutting. **Yield:** 16 servings.

*Editor's Note: This recipe was tested in an 850-watt microwave.*

caramel-chocolate oat squares

For frosting, in a large heavy saucepan, cook butter over medium heat for 5-7 minutes or until golden brown. Pour into a large mixing bowl; beat in the confectioners' sugar, vanilla and enough milk to achieve spreading consistency. Frost bars. **Yield:** about 4 dozen.

## Apricot Bars

Kim Gilliland, Simi Valley, California

These fruit bars have a great flavor. Everyone in my family loves them, and I get lots of requests for the recipe.

```
2/3   cup dried apricots
1/2   cup water
1/2   cup butter, softened
1/4   cup confectioners' sugar
1-1/3 cups all-purpose flour, divided
2     eggs
1     cup packed brown sugar
1/2   teaspoon baking powder
1/4   teaspoon salt
1/2   teaspoon vanilla extract
1/2   cup chopped walnuts
```
Additional confectioners' sugar

In a small saucepan, cook apricots in water over medium heat for 10 minutes or until softened. Drain, cool and chop; set aside. In a mixing bowl, cream butter and confectioners' sugar. Add 1 cup flour; mix until smooth. Press into a greased 8-in. square baking dish. Bake at 350° for 20 minutes or until lightly browned.

Meanwhile, in a mixing bowl, beat eggs and brown sugar. Add the baking powder, salt, vanilla and remaining flour. Stir in apricots and nuts. Pour over crust.

Bake at 350° for 30 minutes or until set. Cool on wire rack. Dust with confectioners' sugar; cut into bars. **Yield:** 16 bars.

frosted pumpkin cranberry bars

## Frosted Pumpkin Cranberry Bars

Barbara Nowakowski, Mesa, Arizona

With tangy dried cranberries tucked inside and a creamy browned butter frosting, these mildly spiced pumpkin bars are doubly delightful. It's a good thing the recipe makes lots, because once you taste one, you won't be able to resist going back for more!

```
1-1/2 cups all-purpose flour
1-1/4 cups sugar
2     teaspoons baking powder
2     teaspoons ground cinnamon
1     teaspoon baking soda
1/2   teaspoon ground ginger
3     eggs
1     can (15 ounces) solid-pack pumpkin
3/4   cup butter, melted
3/4   cup chopped dried cranberries
```
BROWNED BUTTER FROSTING:
```
1/2   cup butter
4     cups confectioners' sugar
1     teaspoon vanilla extract
4     to 6 tablespoons milk
```

In a large bowl, combine the first six ingredients. In another bowl, whisk the eggs, pumpkin and butter; stir into dry ingredients until well combined. Stir in cranberries.

Spread into a greased 15-in. x 10-in. x 1-in. baking pan. Bake at 350° for 20-25 minutes or until a toothpick inserted near the center comes out clean. Cool on a wire rack.

apricot bars

## Sour Cream Raisin Squares

Leona Eash, McConnelsville, Ohio

My aunt shared this recipe with me, and my family has always enjoyed it. I love to make these bars for friends who visit, and I like to give the snacks away as gifts.

      1  cup butter, softened
      1  cup packed brown sugar
      2  cups all-purpose flour
      2  cups quick-cooking oats
      1  teaspoon baking powder
      1  teaspoon baking soda
    1/8  teaspoon salt
**FILLING:**
      4  egg yolks
      2  cups (16 ounces) sour cream
  1-1/2  cups raisins
      1  cup sugar
      1  tablespoon cornstarch

In a large mixing bowl, cream the butter and brown sugar until light and fluffy. Combine the flour, oats, baking powder, baking soda and salt; gradually add to creamed mixture (mixture will be crumbly).

Set aside 2 cups; pat the remaining crumbs into a greased 13-in. x 9-in. x 2-in. baking pan. Bake at 350° for 15 minutes. Cool.

Meanwhile, in a small saucepan, combine filling ingredients. Bring to a boil; cook and stir for 5-8 minutes. Pour over crust; sprinkle with reserved crumbs. Bake 15 minutes longer. **Yield:** 12-16 servings.

sour cream raisin squares

cheesecake squares

## Cheesecake Squares

Shirley Forest, Eau Claire, Wisconsin

I lived on a dairy farm when I was young and my mom always had a lot of sour cream on hand. She never wasted any, and this cheesecake was one of my family's favorites. It's great topped with blackberries.

      2  packages (8 ounces *each*) cream cheese,
         softened
      1  cup ricotta cheese
  1-1/2  cups sugar
      4  eggs
    1/4  cup butter, melted and cooled
      3  tablespoons cornstarch
      3  tablespoons all-purpose flour
      1  tablespoon vanilla extract
      2  cups (16 ounces) sour cream
**Seasonal fresh fruit, optional**

In a large mixing bowl, beat cream cheese, ricotta and sugar until smooth. Add the eggs, one at a time, mixing well after each addition. Beat in the butter, cornstarch, flour and vanilla until smooth. Fold in sour cream.

Pour into a greased 13-in. x 9-in. x 2-in. baking pan. Bake, uncovered, at 325° for 1 hour or until almost set. Cool on a wire rack for 10 minutes. Carefully run a knife around edge of pan to loosen; cool 1 hour longer. Chill several hours or overnight. Top each square with fruit if desired. **Yield:** 20 servings.

## Cappuccino Cake Brownies

Mary Houchin, Lebanon, Illinois

If you like your sweets with a cup of coffee, this recipe is for you! The no-nut brownies combine a mild coffee flavor with the richness of semisweet chocolate chips. They're a quick and easy dessert or anytime treat.

1 tablespoon instant coffee granules
2 teaspoons boiling water
1 cup (6 ounces) semisweet chocolate chips
1/4 cup butter, softened
1/2 cup sugar
2 eggs
1/2 cup all-purpose flour
1/4 teaspoon ground cinnamon

In a small bowl, dissolve coffee in water; set aside. In a microwave, melt chocolate chips; stir until smooth. In a small mixing bowl, cream butter and sugar until light and fluffy. Beat in eggs, melted chocolate and coffee mixture. Combine flour and cinnamon; gradually add to creamed mixture until blended.

Pour into a greased 8-in. square baking pan. Bake at 350° for 25-30 minutes or until a toothpick inserted near the center comes out clean. Cool on a wire rack. Cut into squares. **Yield:** 16 bars.

## Pear Custard Bars

Jeannette Nord, San Juan Capistrano, California

*When I take this crowd-pleasing treat to a potluck, I come home with an empty pan every time.*

1/2 cup butter, softened
1/3 cup sugar
1/4 teaspoon vanilla extract
3/4 cup all-purpose flour
2/3 cup chopped macadamia nuts
FILLING/TOPPING:
1 package (8 ounces) cream cheese, softened
1/2 cup sugar
1 egg

pear custard bars

1/2 teaspoon vanilla extract
1 can (15-1/4 ounces) pear halves, drained
1/2 teaspoon sugar
1/2 teaspoon ground cinnamon

In a large mixing bowl, cream butter and sugar until light and fluffy. Beat in vanilla. Gradually add flour to creamed mixture. Stir in the nuts.

Press into a greased 8-in. square baking pan. Bake at 350° for 20 minutes or until lightly browned. Cool on a wire rack.

In a small mixing bowl, beat cream cheese until smooth. Beat in the sugar, egg and the vanilla. Pour over crust.

Cut pears into 1/8-in. slices; arrange in a single layer over filling. Combine sugar and cinnamon; sprinkle over pears. Bake at 375° for 28-30 minutes (center will be soft set and will become firmer upon cooling). Cool on a wire rack for 45 minutes.

Cover and refrigerate for at least 2 hours before cutting. Store in the refrigerator. **Yield:** 16 bars.

cappuccino cake brownies

## Brownie Point

It's a snap to turn your brownies from ordinary to extraordinary...even if you rely on a boxed mix! Simply stir a handful of chocolate or butterscotch chips into the batter, or add a little mint extract. You can also try replacing some of the water in the recipe with cooled coffee.

apple danish

## Apple Danish

Sandy Lynch, Decatur, Illinois

These are a perfect addition to breakfast or brunch. A friend gave me the recipe for the delightful squares that make good use of our bountiful apple harvest.

PASTRY:
- 3 cups all-purpose flour
- 1/2 teaspoon salt
- 1 cup shortening
- 1 egg yolk
- 1/2 cup milk

FILLING:
- 6 cups sliced peeled apples
- 1-1/2 cups sugar
- 1/4 cup butter, melted
- 2 tablespoons all-purpose flour
- 1 teaspoon ground cinnamon

GLAZE:
- 1 egg white, lightly beaten
- 1/2 cup confectioners' sugar
- 2 to 3 teaspoons water

In a mixing bowl, combine flour and salt; cut in shortening until mixture resembles coarse crumbs. Combine egg yolk and milk; add to flour mixture. Stir just until dough clings together. Divide dough in half.

On a lightly floured surface, roll half of dough into a 15-in. x 10-in. rectangle; transfer to a greased 15-in. x 10-in. x 1-in. baking pan. Set aside.

In a bowl, toss together filling ingredients; spoon over pastry in pan. Roll out remaining dough into another 15-in. x 10-in. rectangle. Place over filling. Brush with egg white. Bake at 375° for 40 minutes or until golden brown. Cool on a wire rack.

For glaze, combine the confectioners' sugar and enough water to achieve a drizzling consistency. Drizzle over warm pastry. Cut into squares. Serve warm or cold. **Yield:** 20-24 servings.

## Honey Pecan Triangles

Debbie Fogel, East Berne, New York

Here are some tasty bars that have all the goodness of pecan pie! Always a big success, the triangles make it easy to serve to a bunch.

- 2 teaspoons plus 1/2 cup butter, softened, *divided*
- 1/2 cup packed brown sugar
- 1 egg yolk
- 1-1/2 cups all-purpose flour

TOPPING:
- 1 cup packed brown sugar
- 1/2 cup butter
- 1/4 cup honey
- 1/2 cup heavy whipping cream
- 4 cups chopped pecans

Line a 13-in. x 9-in. x 2-in. baking pan with foil; butter the foil with 2 teaspoons butter. In a mixing bowl, cream remaining butter with brown sugar. Add egg yolk; mix well. Gradually add flour. Press into prepared pan. Bake at 350° for 15 minutes or until golden brown.

Meanwhile, in a large saucepan, combine the brown sugar, butter and honey. Bring to a boil over medium heat; cook and stir for 3 minutes. Remove from the heat; stir in cream and pecans. Pour over crust. Bake for 30 minutes or until hot and bubbly. Cool completely on a wire rack.

Use foil to lift the bars out of the pan and place on a cutting board. Carefully remove foil. Cut into 24 bars; cut each in half diagonally. **Yield:** 4 dozen.

honey pecan triangles

frosted peanut butter fingers

## Frosted Peanut Butter Fingers

Leah Gallington, Corona, California

I first learned about these quick crowd-pleasers from a next-door neighbor when I sniffed the delightful aroma of a batch baking. Topped with extra peanut butter and chocolate frosting, the chewy bars became a family favorite that day when she brought us a plateful.

|       |                                        |
|-------|----------------------------------------|
| 1     | cup butter, softened                   |
| 1-1/2 | cups packed brown sugar                |
| 1     | cup sugar                              |
| 2-1/2 | cups creamy peanut butter, *divided*   |
| 1     | egg                                    |
| 1-1/2 | teaspoons vanilla extract              |
| 2-1/2 | cups quick-cooking oats                |
| 2     | cups all-purpose flour                 |
| 1     | teaspoon baking soda                   |
| 1/2   | teaspoon salt                          |

CHOCOLATE FROSTING:

|     |                            |
|-----|----------------------------|
| 6   | tablespoons butter, softened |
| 4   | cups confectioners' sugar  |
| 1/2 | cup baking cocoa           |
| 1   | teaspoon vanilla extract   |
| 6   | to 8 tablespoons milk      |

In a large mixing bowl, cream butter and sugars until light and fluffy. Beat in 1 cup peanut butter, egg and vanilla. Combine oats, flour, baking soda and salt; gradually add to creamed mixture.

Spread into a greased 15-in. x 10-in. x 1-in. baking pan. Bake at 350° for 13-17 minutes or until golden brown. Cool slightly on a wire rack, about 12 minutes. Spread with remaining peanut butter. Cool completely.

In a large mixing bowl, beat the butter, confectioners' sugar, cocoa, vanilla and enough milk to achieve spreading consistency. Spread over peanut butter. Cut into bars. **Yield:** about 3 dozen.

*Editor's Note: Reduced-fat or generic brands of peanut butter are not recommended for this recipe.*

## Chocolate Chip Cheesecake Bars

Jane Nolt, Narvon, Pennsylvania

I received this recipe from a co-worker who made these heavenly bars for a potluck. Since they combine two favorite flavors—chocolate chip cookies and cheesecake—in one bite, they were a hit with our three grown children.

|       |                                      |
|-------|--------------------------------------|
| 3/4   | cup shortening                       |
| 3/4   | cup sugar                            |
| 1/3   | cup packed brown sugar               |
| 1     | egg                                  |
| 1-1/2 | teaspoons vanilla extract            |
| 1-1/2 | cups all-purpose flour               |
| 1     | teaspoon salt                        |
| 3/4   | teaspoon baking soda                 |
| 1-1/2 | cups miniature chocolate chips       |
| 3/4   | cup chopped pecans                   |

FILLING:

|     |                                                 |
|-----|-------------------------------------------------|
| 2   | packages (8 ounces *each*) cream cheese, softened |
| 3/4 | cup sugar                                       |
| 2   | eggs                                            |
| 1   | teaspoon vanilla extract                        |

In a large mixing bowl, cream shortening and sugars until light and fluffy. Beat in egg and vanilla. Combine the flour, salt and baking soda; gradually add to the creamed mixture until blended. Fold in the chocolate chips and the pecans.

Set aside a third of the dough for topping. Press remaining dough into a greased 13-in. x 9-in. x 2-in. baking pan. Bake at 350° for 8 minutes.

Meanwhile, in a small mixing bowl, beat cream cheese and sugar until smooth. Beat in eggs and vanilla. Spoon over crust.

Drop teaspoonfuls of reserved dough over filling. Bake at 350° for 35-40 minutes or until golden brown. Cool on a wire rack. Cover and store in the refrigerator. **Yield:** 3 dozen.

chocolate chip cheesecake bars

butterscotch cashew bars

## Butterscotch Cashew Bars

Lori Berg, Wentzville, Missouri

I knew these nutty bars were a success when I took them on our annual family vacation. My husband couldn't stop eating them...and my sister-in-law, who is a great baker, asked for my secret. It makes a big batch, which is good, because they go so quickly!

| | |
|---|---|
| 1 | cup plus 2 tablespoons butter, softened |
| 3/4 | cup plus 2 tablespoons packed brown sugar |
| 2-1/2 | cups all-purpose flour |
| 1-3/4 | teaspoons salt |

TOPPING:

| | |
|---|---|
| 1 | package (10 to 11 ounces) butterscotch chips |
| 1/2 | cup plus 2 tablespoons light corn syrup |
| 3 | tablespoons butter |
| 2 | teaspoons water |
| 2-1/2 | cups salted cashew halves |

## Brownie Point

Always test brownies for doneness toward the end of the baking time. If the brownies spring back when lightly touched in the center and the sides have started to pull away from the pan, the batch is done. Cake-like brownies are done when a toothpick inserted near the center comes out clean.

In a large mixing bowl, cream the butter and brown sugar until light and fluffy. Combine flour and salt; add to creamed mixture just until combined.

Press into a greased 15-in. x 10-in. x 1-in. baking pan. Bake at 350° for 10-12 minutes or until lightly browned.

Meanwhile, in a small saucepan, combine the butterscotch chips, corn syrup, butter and water. Cook and stir over medium heat until the chips and butter are melted.

Spread over crust. Sprinkle with cashews; press down lightly. Bake for 11-13 minutes or until topping is bubbly and lightly browned. Cool on a wire rack. Cut into bars. **Yield:** 3-1/2 dozen.

## Moist Cake Brownies

Louise Stacey, Dane, Wisconsin

These brownies have been in my collection since I was 9 years old. I've added to and altered the recipe over the years, and now I think it has the perfect amount of everything, including semisweet and milk chocolate chips and pecans. They are my husband's and son's most requested treat by far!

| | |
|---|---|
| 2/3 | cup butter, cubed |
| 3/4 | cup baking cocoa |
| 1/4 | cup vegetable oil |
| 2 | cups sugar |
| 4 | eggs |
| 2 | teaspoons vanilla extract |
| 1-1/2 | cups all-purpose flour |
| 1 | teaspoon baking powder |
| 1 | teaspoon salt |
| 2/3 | cup semisweet chocolate chips |
| 1/2 | cup milk chocolate chips |

moist cake brownies

banana cream brownie dessert

1 cup coarsely chopped pecans
Confectioners' sugar
Pecan halves, toasted, optional

Melt butter in a large saucepan. Whisk in cocoa and oil until smooth. Cook and stir over low heat until cocoa is blended. Transfer to a large bowl; stir in sugar. Add eggs, one at a time, stirring well after each addition. Stir in vanilla. Combine flour, baking powder and salt; gradually add to cocoa mixture. Stir in the chocolate chips and nuts.

Spread into a greased 13-in. x 9-in. x 2-in. baking pan. Bake at 350° for 25-30 minutes or until a toothpick inserted near the center comes out clean. Cool in pan on a wire rack. Dust with confectioners' sugar. Garnish with pecan halves if desired. **Yield:** 2 dozen.

## Banana Cream Brownie Dessert

Julie Nowakowski, LaSalle, Illinois

I always keep the ingredients for this extremely delicious brownie dessert on hand because I make it quite often for potlucks and family gatherings. I'm always asked for the recipe. After one bite, you'll understand why.

1 package fudge brownie mix (13-inch x 9-inch pan size)
1 cup (6 ounces) semisweet chocolate chips, *divided*
3/4 cup dry roasted peanuts, chopped, *divided*
3 medium firm bananas
1-2/3 cups cold milk
2 packages (5.1 ounces *each)* instant vanilla pudding mix
1 carton (8 ounces) frozen whipped topping, thawed

Prepare brownie batter according to package directions for fudge-like brownies. Stir in 1/2 cup chocolate chips and 1/4 cup peanuts. Spread into a greased 13-in. x 9-in. x 2-in. baking pan. Bake at 350° for 28-30 minutes or until a toothpick inserted near the center comes out clean. Cool on a wire rack.

Slice bananas; arrange in a single layer over brownies. Chop the remaining chocolate chips. Sprinkle 1/4 cup chopped chips and 1/4 cup peanuts over bananas.

In a large mixing bowl, beat the milk and pudding mixes on low speed for 2 minutes. Fold in whipped topping. Spread over the top. Sprinkle with the remaining chips and the pecans. Refrigerate leftovers. **Yield:** 12-15 servings.

## Chocolate Crunch Brownies

Pat Mueller, Mitchell, South Dakota

The first time I took these to work, I knew I'd better start making copies of the recipe—they disappeared fast!

1 cup butter, softened
2 cups sugar
4 eggs
6 tablespoons baking cocoa
1 cup all-purpose flour
2 teaspoons vanilla extract
1/2 teaspoon salt
1 jar (7 ounces) marshmallow creme
1 cup creamy peanut butter
2 cups (12 ounces) semisweet chocolate chips
3 cups crisp rice cereal

In a large mixing bowl, cream butter and sugar until fluffy. Beat in eggs and vanilla. Combine the flour, cocoa and salt; gradually add to creamed mixture.

Spread into a greased 13-in. x 9-in. x 2-in. baking pan. Bake at 350° for 25 minutes or until brownies test done. Cool in pan on a wire rack. Spread marshmallow creme over cooled brownies.

In a small saucepan, melt peanut butter and chocolate chips over low heat, stirring constantly until smooth. Remove from the heat; stir in the cereal and toss to coat. Spread over marshmallow layer. Chill before cutting. Store in refrigerator. **Yield:** 3 dozen.

chocolate crunch brownies

# Chapter 2

p. 31

p. 23

p. 24

p. 27

p. 30

# Chocolate Sensations

If it's chocolate you crave, the following recipes are just for you! Jam-packed with decadent, chocolaty specialties, this chapter is surely every chocoholic's dream come true.

## Fudgy Walnut Brownies

Diane Truver, Valencia, Pennsylvania

We have lots of great cooks in our clan, so adding to our collection of family recipes is a tradition. I came up with these moist, nut-covered brownies while doing my holiday baking. Now everyone requests them.

- 3/4 cup butter, cubed
- 4 squares (1 ounce *each*) unsweetened chocolate
- 4 eggs
- 2 cups sugar
- 1 teaspoon vanilla extract
- 1 cup all-purpose flour

WALNUT CRUNCH TOPPING:
- 3/4 cup packed brown sugar
- 1/4 cup butter, cubed
- 2 eggs, lightly beaten
- 2 tablespoons all-purpose flour
- 1 teaspoon vanilla extract
- 4 cups chopped walnuts

In a microwave, melt butter and chocolate; stir until smooth. Cool slightly. In a large bowl, beat eggs and sugar; stir in vanilla and chocolate mixture. Stir in flour until well blended. Pour into a greased 13-in. x 9-in. x 2-in. baking pan; set aside.

For topping, in a small saucepan, combine brown sugar and butter. Cook and stir over low heat until butter is melted. Stir in the eggs, flour and vanilla until well blended. Stir in nuts.

Spread evenly over brownie batter. Bake at 350° for 40-45 minutes or until a toothpick inserted near the center comes out with moist crumbs (do not overbake). Cool completely on a wire rack. **Yield:** 1-1/2 dozen.

fudgy walnut brownies

german chocolate bars

## German Chocolate Bars

Jennifer Sharp, Murfreesboro, Tennessee

My mom gave me this recipe when I wanted to surprise friends with something different and yummy. The bars can be cut into larger pieces, but they're very rich.

- 1 package (18-1/4 ounces) German chocolate cake mix
- 2/3 cup cold butter
- 1 cup (6 ounces) semisweet chocolate chips
- 1 can (15 ounces) coconut-pecan frosting
- 1/4 cup milk

Place cake mix in a large bowl; cut in butter until crumbly. Press 2-1/2 cups into a greased 13-in. x 9-in. x 2-in. baking pan. Bake at 350° for 10 minutes; immediately sprinkle with chocolate chips. Drop frosting by tablespoonfuls over the chips.

Stir milk into the remaining crumb mixture; drop by teaspoonfuls over top. Bake 25-30 minutes longer or until bubbly around the edges and top is cracked. Cool on a wire rack. Refrigerate for 4 hours before cutting. **Yield:** 4 dozen.

## Triple-Chocolate Brownie Squares

Kathy Fannoun, Brooklyn Park, Minnesota

Featuring a chocolate-pudding layer, a frosting of whipped topping and chocolate chips, these refrigerator brownies simply can't be beat!

- 1 package brownie mix (13-inch x 9-inch pan size)
- 1-1/2 cups milk
- 1 package (1.4 ounces) sugar-free instant chocolate pudding mix
- 1/4 cup hot fudge ice cream topping
- 1/4 cup plus 1 tablespoon miniature semisweet chocolate chips, *divided*
- 4 cups frozen whipped topping, thawed, *divided*

Prepare and bake brownies according to package directions, using a 13-in. x 9-in. x 2-in. baking pan coated with nonstick cooking spray. Cool on a wire rack.

Meanwhile, in a large mixing bowl, beat milk and dry pudding mix for 2 minutes or until slightly thickened. Beat in fudge topping until blended.

In a microwave, melt 1/4 cup chocolate chips; stir until smooth. Beat into pudding mixture. Fold in 2 cups whipped topping. Spread over cooled brownies. Cover and refrigerate until pudding is set. Spread with remaining whipped topping. Sprinkle with remaining chocolate chips. **Yield:** 15 servings.

## Simply Fudgy Brownies

Marjorie Hoyt, Center Conway, New Hampshire

I don't know where I got this recipe, but I've had it for over 30 years—it's written on an old, yellow piece of paper. Adding chocolate chips was my idea. When my children were in school, I found out they were actually selling these brownies to their friends!

|       |                         |
|-------|-------------------------|
| 1/4   | cup baking cocoa        |
| 1/2   | cup vegetable oil       |
| 2     | eggs                    |
| 1     | cup sugar               |
| 1     | teaspoon vanilla extract|
| 3/4   | cup all-purpose flour   |
| 1/8   | teaspoon salt           |
| 1/2   | cup chopped walnuts     |
| 1/2   | cup milk chocolate chips|

In a small bowl, combine cocoa and oil until smooth. In another bowl, beat eggs. Add the sugar, vanilla and cocoa mixture. Stir in flour and salt just until moistened. Fold in walnuts.

Pour into a greased 8-in. square baking pan; sprinkle with chocolate chips. Bake at 325° for 30 minutes or until a toothpick inserted near the center comes out clean. Cool on a wire rack. **Yield:** 16 brownies.

marbled chocolate bars

## Marbled Chocolate Bars

Margery Bryan, Royal City, Washington

With only four ingredients, these scrumptious chocolate bars with pockets of rich cream cheese are perfect for taking to a potluck. They're quick to assemble, don't need frosting and are easy to transport and serve. Best of all, folks love them!

|       |                                              |
|-------|----------------------------------------------|
| 1     | package (18-1/4 ounces) German chocolate cake mix |
| 1     | package (8 ounces) cream cheese, softened    |
| 1/2   | cup sugar                                    |
| 3/4   | cup milk chocolate chips, *divided*          |

Prepare cake batter according to package directions. Pour into a greased 15-in. x 10-in. x 1-in. baking pan. In a small mixing bowl, beat cream cheese and sugar until smooth. Stir in 1/4 cup chocolate chips. Drop by tablespoonfuls over batter. Cut through batter with a knife to swirl the cream cheese mixture. Sprinkle with remaining chocolate chips.

Bake at 350° for 25-30 minutes or until a toothpick inserted near the center comes out clean. Cool on a wire rack. Cut into bars. **Yield:** 3 dozen.

simply fudgy brownies

## Brownie Point

Packaged brownie mixes are a great way to prepare treats at a moment's notice. If you live in a high altitude, you likely know that adding extra flour to a mix helps improve the final dessert. Next time, add a little cocoa powder instead and you'll have extra chocolaty brownies.

really rocky road brownies

## Really Rocky Road Brownies

Brenda Wood, Egbert, Ontario

Rocky road usually refers to any kind of dessert featuring nuts, marshmallows and chocolate. It's so named because of a "rocky road" appearance, which these snacks offer.

       8  squares (1 ounce *each*) unsweetened chocolate
 1-1/2  cups butter
       6  eggs
       3  cups sugar
       1  tablespoon vanilla extract
 1-1/2  cups all-purpose flour
       1  cup chopped walnuts, optional
TOPPING:
       2  cups miniature marshmallows
       1  square (1 ounce) unsweetened chocolate, melted

In a heavy saucepan or microwave, melt chocolate and butter; stir until smooth. Cool slightly. In a large mixing bowl, beat eggs for 2 minutes. Gradually add sugar; beating until thick and pale yellow, about 3 minutes. Stir in chocolate mixture and vanilla. Fold in flour and nuts if desired.

Pour into two greased and floured 9-in. square baking pans. Bake at 350° for 25-30 minutes or until a toothpick inserted in the center comes out with moist crumbs (do not overbake). Sprinkle each pan with 1 cup of marshmallows. Broil until marshmallows are golden brown, about 30-60 seconds. Drizzle with melted chocolate. Cool on a wire rack. Refrigerate for several hours before cutting. **Yield:** 4 dozen.

## Sweet Chocolate Bars

Linda Binger, Taylorville, Illinois

Using a refrigerated pizza crust saves time when preparing this sweet treat. Loaded with chocolate chips, coconut and nuts, the chewy bars are extra rich and tasty.

       1  tube (13.8 ounces) refrigerated pizza crust
 1-1/2  cups semisweet chocolate chips
    1/2  cup chopped pecans
    1/2  cup flaked coconut
       1  can (14 ounces) sweetened condensed milk
       1  package (7-1/2 ounces) white frosting mix
    1/2  cup butter, melted

Press pizza dough onto the bottom of a greased 13-in. x 9-in. x 2-in. baking pan. Sprinkle with chocolate chips, pecans and coconut. Drizzle with milk. Sprinkle with dry frosting mix. Drizzle with butter.

Bake at 350° for 35-40 minutes or until golden brown. Cool on a wire rack for 10 minutes; run a knife around edges. Cool completely before cutting. **Yield:** 4-1/2 dozen.

*Editor's Note:* This recipe was tested with Jiffy dry frosting mix.

## Fudge-Filled Bars

Renee Zimmer, Gig Harbor, Washington

I appreciate the ease of baking these oat bars on a busy day, and our children love their fudgy filling. With colorful candies on top, the sweet squares are sure to sell at bake sales.

       2  cups quick-cooking oats
 1-1/2  cups all-purpose flour
       1  cup packed brown sugar
    3/4  teaspoon salt
       1  cup butter, melted
       1  cup chopped pecans
       1  can (14 ounces) sweetened condensed milk
       1  cup (6 ounces) semisweet chocolate chips
       2  tablespoons shortening
       1  cup milk chocolate M&M's

In a large bowl, combine the oats, flour, brown sugar and salt. Add butter and mix until crumbly. Stir in the pecans. Set aside 1-1/2 cups for topping. Press remaining crumb mixture into a greased 13-in. x 9-in. x 2-in. baking pan.

In a large saucepan, combine the milk, chocolate chips and shortening. Cook and stir over low heat until chips are melted; stir until smooth.

Spread over crust; sprinkle with the reserved crumb mixture. Top with M&M's. Bake at 350° for 20-25 minutes or until edges are golden brown. **Yield:** 2-1/2 dozen.

fudge-filled bars

## German Chocolate Cheesecake Bars

Jerry Minerich, Westminster, Colorado

Here's a great treat that combines cheesecake with the wonderful flavor of German chocolate in a dessert bar. Made from scratch, the squares are worth the wait.

- 1 package (1/4 ounce) active dry yeast
- 1/2 cup warm water (110° to 115°)
- 1/4 cup sugar
- 1/2 teaspoon salt
- 1 egg
- 1/2 cup butter, softened
- 2 to 2-1/2 cups all-purpose flour

**FILLING:**
- 2 packages (8 ounces *each*) cream cheese, softened
- 1/3 cup baking cocoa
- 1 cup sugar
- 3 eggs
- 2 teaspoons vanilla extract

**TOPPING:**
- 1/2 cup sugar
- 1 egg
- 1/2 cup evaporated milk
- 1/4 cup butter
- 1 teaspoon vanilla extract
- 2/3 cup flaked coconut
- 1/2 cup chopped pecans

In a large mixing bowl, dissolve yeast in water. Add sugar, salt, egg, butter and 1 cup of flour; beat until smooth. Add enough remaining flour to form a soft dough.

Turn onto a floured surface; knead until smooth and elastic, about 3-5 minutes. Place in a greased bowl, turning once to grease top. Cover and let rest for 20 minutes.

Punch dough down. Press into the bottom and up the sides of a greased 15-in. x 10-in. x 1-in. baking pan. In a large mixing bowl, beat cream cheese until smooth; gradually add cocoa and sugar. Beat until fluffy. Beat in eggs, one at a time. Add vanilla. Pour into crust. Bake at 350° for 20-25 minutes or until crust is golden brown; cool.

In a saucepan, combine first four topping ingredients; cook over low heat until thick, about 8-10 minutes, stirring constantly. Remove from heat; stir in vanilla, coconut and nuts. Spread over cooled cake. Chill at least 1 hour. Store in the refrigerator. **Yield:** 3 dozen.

## Layered Brownies

Sharon Miller, Elkhart, Indiana

I have always enjoyed cooking and baking. Now I have grandchildren that like to help me in the kitchen. These chocolaty bars are one of our favorites.

- 1 package (18-1/4 ounces) chocolate cake mix
- 1 cup chopped nuts
- 1/3 cup vegetable oil
- 1 egg
- 1 can (14 ounces) sweetened condensed milk

chocolate oatmeal bars

- 1 cup (6 ounces) semisweet chocolate chips
- 1/8 teaspoon salt
- 1 teaspoon vanilla extract

In a large mixing bowl, combine the cake mix, nuts, oil and egg until crumbly. Set aside 1-1/2 cups for topping. Press the remaining crumb mixture into a greased 13-in. x 9-in. x 2-in. baking pan.

In a saucepan, combine milk, chocolate chips and salt. Cook and stir over low heat until chips are melted. Stir in vanilla. Spread evenly in pan. Sprinkle with reserved crumb mixture.

Bake at 350° for 25-30 minutes or until a toothpick inserted near the center comes out clean. Cool on a wire rack. **Yield:** 4 dozen.

## Chocolate Oatmeal Bars

Mary Ann Meredith, Pittsford, Michigan

I made this dessert for eight ladies who recently stayed at our bed-and-breakfast, and they just raved about it. An oat crust is topped with chocolate and peanut butter, then sprinkled with crushed toffee candy bars.

- 1/3 cup butter, softened
- 1 cup packed brown sugar
- 1/3 cup corn syrup
- 1 teaspoon vanilla extract
- 4 cups quick-cooking oats
- 1 package (11-1/2 ounces) milk chocolate chips
- 2/3 cup chunky peanut butter
- 4 Heath candy bars (1.4 ounces *each*), crushed

In a mixing bowl, cream the butter and brown sugar until light and fluffy. Beat in corn syrup and vanilla. Stir in oats; press into a greased 13-in. x 9-in. x 2-in. baking pan.

Bake at 350° for 12-15 minutes or until golden brown. Cool on a wire rack.

In a microwave, melt chocolate chips and peanut butter; stir until blended. Spread over cooled bars. Sprinkle with crushed candy bars. Chill until set; cut into bars. **Yield:** 3 dozen.

## Crispy Fudge Treats

Joyce Jackson, Bridgetown, Nova Scotia

These yummy bars keep well in the fridge, but I never have to store them for very long!

    6   cups crisp rice cereal
    3/4 cup confectioners' sugar
    1-3/4 cups semisweet chocolate chips
    1/2 cup corn syrup
    1/3 cup butter
    2   teaspoons vanilla extract

In a large bowl, combine cereal and sugar; set aside. Place the chocolate chips, corn syrup and butter in a 1-qt. microwave-safe dish. Microwave, uncovered, on high for about 1 minute; stir gently until smooth. Stir in vanilla. Pour over cereal mixture; toss to coat.

Spoon into a greased 13-in. x 9-in. x 2-in. baking pan. Refrigerate for 30 minutes; cut into squares. Store in the refrigerator. **Yield:** 3 dozen.

fudge brownies

## Chocolate Chip Brownies

Beverly Wilkerson, Crocker, Missouri

We call these "magic bars" because they are fast and easy to make, and they disappear quickly when they are finished...just like magic!

    2   tubes (18 ounces *each*) refrigerated chocolate
        chip cookie dough
    3/4 cup flaked coconut, *divided*
    1   package brownie mix (8-inch square pan size)
    1/2 cup semisweet chocolate chips
    1/2 cup chopped pecans

Press cookie dough into a greased 13-in. x 9-in. x 2-in. baking pan. Sprinkle with 1/2 cup coconut and press firmly into dough.

Prepare brownie mix according to package directions; spread batter over coconut. Sprinkle with remaining coconut; top with chocolate chips and pecans.

Bake at 350° for 45-50 minutes or until a toothpick inserted near the center comes out clean (do not over-bake). Cool on a wire rack. **Yield:** 2 dozen.

chocolate chip brownies

## Fudge Brownies

Hazel Fritchie, Palestine, Illinois

My children always looked forward to these after-school snacks. They're so fudgy, they don't even need icing.

    1   cup butter
    6   squares (1 ounce *each*) unsweetened chocolate
    4   eggs
    2   cups sugar
    1   teaspoon vanilla extract
    1/2 teaspoon salt
    1   cup all-purpose flour
    2   cups chopped walnuts
Confectioners' sugar, optional

In a small saucepan, melt butter and chocolate over low heat; cool for 10 minutes. In a large mixing bowl, beat the eggs, sugar, vanilla and salt. Stir in the chocolate mixture. Add flour and nuts; mix well.

Pour into a greased 11-in. x 7-in. x 2-in. baking dish. Bake at 325° for 45-50 minutes or until a toothpick inserted near the center comes out with moist crumbs. Cool on a wire rack. Dust with confectioners' sugar if desired. Cut into bars. **Yield:** 16 servings.

## Chocolate Cheesecake Squares

Helen Longmire, Austin, Texas

These bite-size bars are very rich, so small servings are satisfying. They're perfect for parties because they don't require a fork and plate to eat.

    1   cup all-purpose flour
    1/2 cup sugar
    3   tablespoons baking cocoa
    1   teaspoon baking powder
    1/4 teaspoon salt
    1/2 cup cold butter

friendship brownies

1  egg yolk
1  teaspoon vanilla extract
1/2  cup finely chopped walnuts
FILLING:
1  package (8 ounces) cream cheese, softened
1/3  cup sugar
1/2  cup sour cream
1  tablespoon all-purpose flour
2  teaspoons grated orange peel
1/4  teaspoon salt
1  egg
1  egg white
1/2  teaspoon vanilla extract
Chocolate sprinkles, optional

Line a 9-in. square baking pan with foil; grease the foil and set aside. In a large bowl, combine the first five ingredients. Cut in butter until fine crumbs form. Stir in the egg yolk, vanilla and walnuts.

Press onto the bottom of prepared pan. Bake at 325° for 15 minutes.

In a small mixing bowl, beat cream cheese and sugar until smooth. Beat in the sour cream, flour, orange peel and salt. Beat in the egg, egg white and vanilla on low speed just until combined.

Pour over warm crust. Bake for 20-25 minutes or until center is almost set. Cool on a wire rack for 1 hour.

Garnish top with chocolate sprinkles if desired. Refrigerate overnight. Lift out of the pan; remove foil. Cut into 1-in. squares. **Yield:** 25 servings.

## Mocha Brownies

Suzanne Strocsher, Bothell, Washington

My husband doesn't drink coffee, but he loves the taste of these delightful brownies.

1  package fudge brownie mix (13-inch x 9-inch pan size)
1/2  cup water
1/4  cup vegetable oil
1  egg
2  teaspoons instant coffee granules
1  teaspoon vanilla extract
FILLING:
1/4  cup butter, softened
1/2  cup packed brown sugar
1  egg
2  teaspoons instant coffee granules
1  teaspoon vanilla extract
1  cup chopped walnuts
3/4  cup semisweet chocolate chips
ICING:
1/2  cup semisweet chocolate chips
1  tablespoon butter
1/4  teaspoon instant coffee granules
1  to 2 teaspoons milk

In a large bowl, combine the first six ingredients. Spread into a greased 13-in. x 9-in. x 2-in. baking pan. Bake at 350° for 30-35 minutes or until a toothpick inserted near the center comes out clean (do not overbake).

Meanwhile, in a small mixing bowl, cream butter

and sugar until light and fluffy. Beat in the egg, coffee and vanilla until well blended. Stir in walnuts and chocolate chips. Spread over brownies. Bake at 350° for 17 minutes or until set. Cool on a wire rack.

For icing, in a small saucepan melt the chocolate chips and butter over low heat until chips are melted, stirring constantly. Whisk in coffee and enough milk to reach a drizzling consistency. Drizzle over warm brownies. Cool before cutting. **Yield:** 3 dozen.

## Friendship Brownies

Travis Burkholder, Middleburg, Pennsylvania

Layered in a jar, this brownie mix is the perfect gift to give friends and family during the holidays.

BROWNIE MIX:
1  cup plus 2 tablespoons all-purpose flour
2/3  cup packed brown sugar
3/4  teaspoon salt
2/3  cup sugar
1  teaspoon baking powder
1/3  cup baking cocoa
1/2  cup semisweet chocolate chips
1/2  cup chopped walnuts
ADDITIONAL INGREDIENTS:
3  eggs
2/3  cup vegetable oil
1  teaspoon vanilla extract

Pour the flour into a 1-qt. glass container with a tight-fitting lid. On top of the flour, layer the brown sugar, salt, sugar, baking powder, cocoa, chocolate chips and nuts (do not mix). Cover and store in a cool dry place for up to 6 months. To prepare brownies: In a large bowl, beat the eggs, oil and vanilla. Stir in the brownie mix until well combined.

Spread into a greased 9-in. square baking pan. Bake at 350° for 34-38 minutes or until a toothpick inserted near the center comes out clean. Cool on a wire rack. **Yield:** 16 brownies.

marble chocolate cheesecake bars

## Marble Chocolate Cheesecake Bars

Jean Komlos, Plymouth, Michigan

Chocolate and cream cheese are swirled in these yummy bars to create a sensation that's sure to please your sweet tooth...and fool it at the same time! This dessert tastes so rich, it's hard to believe it's actually low in fat.

        3/4     cup water
        1/3     cup butter
       1-1/2    squares (1-1/2 ounces) unsweetened chocolate
         2      cups all-purpose flour
       1-1/2    cups packed brown sugar
         1      teaspoon baking soda
        1/2     teaspoon salt
         1      egg
         1      egg white
        1/2     cup reduced-fat sour cream
    CREAM CHEESE MIXTURE:
         1      package (8 ounces) reduced-fat cream cheese
        1/3     cup sugar
         1      egg white
         1      tablespoon vanilla extract
         1      cup (6 ounces) miniature semisweet chocolate
                chips

In a small saucepan, combine the water, butter and chocolate. Cook and stir over low heat until melted; stir until smooth. Cool.

   In a large mixing bowl, combine the flour, brown sugar, baking soda and salt. Beat in the egg, egg white and sour cream on low speed just until combined. Beat in chocolate mixture until smooth. In another mixing bowl, beat the cream cheese, sugar, egg white and vanilla until smooth; set aside.

   Spread chocolate batter into a 15-in. x 10-in. x 1-in. baking pan coated with nonstick cooking spray. Drop the cream cheese mixture by tablespoonfuls over batter; cut through batter with a knife to swirl. Sprinkle with chocolate chips.

   Bake at 375° for 20-25 minutes or until a toothpick inserted near the center comes out clean. Cool on a wire rack. **Yield:** about 4 dozen.

## Toffee Bars

Ruth Burrus, Zionsville, Indiana

These shortbread treats feature chocolate bars and have the taste of toffee without the hassle of making candy. They're an attractive addition to a cookie tray.

         1      cup butter, softened
         1      cup packed brown sugar
         1      egg yolk
         1      teaspoon vanilla extract
         2      cups all-purpose flour
        1/4     teaspoon salt
         6      milk chocolate candy bars (1.55 ounces *each*)
        1/2     cup finely chopped pecans

In a large mixing bowl, cream butter and brown sugar until light and fluffy. Beat in egg yolk and vanilla. Gradually add flour and salt, beating until smooth.

   Press into a greased 15-in. x 10-in. x 1-in. baking pan. Bake at 350° for 17-19 minutes or until light golden brown. Immediately place chocolate bars on top; return to the oven for 1 minute. Spread melted chocolate over bars; sprinkle with pecans. **Yield:** about 4 dozen.

## Swiss Chocolate Bars

Margaret Jelinek, Wrentham, Massachusetts

For decadent, chocolate brownies at their best, give these heavenly sensations a try! Topped with a creamy frosting and pecan halves, the rich bars disappear in a flash.

         2      cups all-purpose flour
         2      cups sugar
         1      teaspoon baking soda
        1/2     teaspoon salt
         2      eggs, lightly beaten
        1/2     cup sour cream
         1      cup water
        1/2     cup butter, cubed
       1-1/2    squares (1-1/2 ounces) unsweetened chocolate

swiss chocolate bars

marshmallow brownies

In a large saucepan, melt butterscotch chips and butter over low heat; cool for 10 minutes.

In a large mixing bowl, beat the eggs, brown sugar and vanilla until blended. Beat in butterscotch mixture. Combine the flour, baking powder and salt; add to batter and beat until well blended. Stir in the marshmallows, chocolate chips and nuts.

Spread into a greased 13-in. x 9-in. x 2-in. baking pan. Bake at 325° for 25-30 minutes or until a toothpick inserted near the center comes out clean (do not overbake). Cool completely on a wire rack. **Yield:** 3 dozen.

## Fudgy Brownies

Judy Cunningham, Max, North Dakota

I love to bake treats like these brownies to share with co-workers. When I was growing up, I always helped my mother make delicious, hearty meals and desserts like this for our farm family of eight.

        1-1/3   cups butter, softened
        2-2/3   cups sugar
            4   eggs
            1   tablespoon vanilla extract
            2   cups all-purpose flour
            1   cup baking cocoa
          1/2   teaspoon salt
Confectioners' sugar, optional

In a large mixing bowl, cream butter and sugar until light and fluffy. Beat in eggs and vanilla. Combine flour, cocoa and salt; gradually add to the creamed mixture until well blended.

Spread into a greased 13-in. x 9-in. x 2-in. baking pan. Bake at 350° for 25-30 minutes or until the top is dry and the center is set. Cool completely. Dust with confectioners' sugar if desired. **Yield:** 2-1/2 dozen.

FROSTING:
        4   cups confectioners' sugar
      1/2   cup butter, cubed
      1/3   cup milk
    1-1/2   squares (1-1/2 ounces) unsweetened chocolate
        1   teaspoon vanilla extract
Pecan halves

In a large bowl, combine the flour, sugar, baking soda and salt. In a small bowl, combine eggs and sour cream. In a small saucepan, cook and stir water, butter and chocolate just until melted. Stir into dry ingredients. Stir in sour cream mixture until well blended.

Pour into a greased 15-in. x 10-in. x 1-in. baking pan. Bake at 375° for 25 minutes or until a toothpick inserted near the center comes out clean. Cool on a wire rack for 30 minutes.

Meanwhile, for frosting, place confectioner's sugar in a large mixing bowl; set aside.

In a small saucepan combine the butter, milk and chocolate. Bring to a boil, stirring constantly. Beat into confectioner's sugar until smooth. Stir in vanilla. Let stand for 5 minutes. Spread over warm bars. Top with pecan halves. Cool completely before cutting into bars. **Yield:** about 3 dozen.

## Marshmallow Brownies

Renee Schwebach, Dumont, Minnesota

Picnickers of all ages will love these delightful bars loaded with all sorts of goodies!

        1   cup (6 ounces) butterscotch chips
      1/2   cup butter, cubed
        2   eggs
      2/3   cup packed brown sugar
        1   teaspoon vanilla extract
    1-1/2   cups all-purpose flour
        2   teaspoons baking powder
      1/2   teaspoon salt
        2   cups miniature marshmallows
        2   cups (12 ounces) semisweet chocolate chips
      1/2   cup chopped walnuts

fudgy brownies

## Marble Brownies

Diana Coppernoll, Linden, North Carolina

I like to bake and enjoy trying new recipes, and the cream cheese topping in these microwaved delights made them a fast favorite in my house.

        5   tablespoons butter
        2   squares (1 ounce *each*) unsweetened chocolate
    2/3   cup sugar
        2   eggs
        1   teaspoon vanilla extract
    2/3   cup all-purpose flour
    1/2   teaspoon baking powder
**CHEESECAKE LAYER:**
        1   package (8 ounces) cream cheese
    1/2   cup sugar
        1   egg
        1   teaspoon vanilla extract
        1   cup (6 ounces) semisweet chocolate chips

In a large microwave-safe bowl, combine butter and chocolate. Cover and microwave on high for 30-60 seconds; stir until smooth. Beat in sugar, eggs and vanilla. Stir in flour and baking powder until blended. Spread into a greased microwave-safe 8-in. square dish; set aside.

In a large microwave-safe bowl, heat cream cheese on high for 30-45 seconds or until softened; stir until smooth. Beat in sugar, egg and vanilla. Spoon over brownie batter; cut through batter with a knife to swirl. Sprinkle with chocolate chips.

Shield corners of dish with triangles of foil. Place the dish on an inverted microwave-safe saucer. Cook, uncovered, at 70% power for 8-10 minutes or until a toothpick comes out clean, rotating a half turn after 5 minutes. Heat on high for 1 minute. Remove to a wire rack to cool completely. Store in the refrigerator. **Yield:** 1 dozen.

*Editor's Note: Shielding with small pieces of foil prevents overcooking of food in the corners of a square or rectangular dish. Secure foil firmly to dish and do not allow it to touch insides of the oven.*

*Editor's Note: This recipe was tested in a 1,100-watt microwave.*

marble brownies

chocolate maple bars

## Chocolate Maple Bars

Cathy Schumacher, Alto, Michigan

I use real maple syrup in this bar recipe. The goodies disappear quickly wherever I take them.

    1/2   cup shortening
    3/4   cup maple syrup
    1/2   cup sugar
        3   eggs
        3   tablespoons milk
        1   teaspoon vanilla extract
    1-1/4   cups all-purpose flour
    1/4   teaspoon baking powder
    1/4   teaspoon salt
    1-1/2   squares (1-1/2 ounces) unsweetened
            chocolate, melted
    1/2   cup chopped pecans
    1/2   cup flaked coconut
**FROSTING:**
    1/4   cup butter, softened
        1   cup confectioners' sugar
    1/2   cup baking cocoa
    1/2   cup maple syrup
        1   cup miniature marshmallows

In a large mixing bowl, cream the shortening, syrup and sugar until light and fluffy. Beat in the eggs, milk and vanilla. Combine the flour, baking powder and salt; add to creamed mixture until well combined. Remove half of the batter to another bowl.

Combine melted chocolate and pecans; stir into one of the bowls. Spread into a greased 13-in. x 9-in. x 2-in. baking pan. Add coconut to remaining batter. Spread carefully over chocolate batter.

Bake at 350° for 25 minutes or until a toothpick inserted near the center comes out clean. Cool completely on a wire rack.

For frosting, in a small mixing bowl, beat butter until smooth. Gradually add the confectioners' sugar and cocoa. Gradually add syrup, beating until smooth. Fold in marshmallows. Frost bars. **Yield:** 3 dozen.

## Rich Chocolate Brownies

Karen Trapp, North Weymouth, Massachusetts

I'm one of those people who need chocolate on a regular basis. I looked high and low for a rich brownie recipe that called for cocoa instead of chocolate squares and this is it. My family loves these brownies—they never last more than a day.

      1    cup sugar
      2    eggs
    1/2    teaspoon vanilla extract
    1/2    cup butter, melted
    1/2    cup all-purpose flour
    1/3    cup baking cocoa
    1/4    teaspoon baking powder
    1/4    teaspoon salt
  FROSTING:
      3    tablespoons baking cocoa
      3    tablespoons butter, melted
      2    tablespoons warm water
      1    teaspoon instant coffee granules
  1-1/2    cups confectioners' sugar

In a large mixing bowl, beat the sugar, eggs and vanilla. Add butter; mix well. Combine the flour, cocoa, baking powder and salt; add to batter and mix well.

Pour into a greased 8-in. square baking dish. Bake at 350° for 25-30 minutes or until a toothpick inserted near the center comes out clean. Cool on a wire rack.

For frosting, combine the cocoa and butter. Combine the water and coffee granules; add to cocoa mixture. Stir in sugar until smooth. Frost brownies. **Yield:** 12 servings.

## Double Chocolate Bars

Nancy Clark, Zeigler, Illinois

A friend brought these fudgy bars a few years ago to tempt me with yet another chocolate treat. They are simple to make...and cleanup is a breeze! They're very rich, though, so be sure to cut them into bite-size pieces.

rich chocolate brownies

brownie mounds

      1    package (16 ounces) cream-filled chocolate
           sandwich cookies, crushed
    3/4    cup butter, melted
      1    can (14 ounces) sweetened condensed milk
      2    cups (12 ounces) miniature semisweet
           chocolate chips, *divided*

Combine cookie crumbs and butter; pat onto the bottom of an ungreased 13-in. x 9-in. x 2-in. baking pan. Combine milk and 1 cup of chips in a microwave-safe bowl. Cover and microwave on high for 30 seconds or until chips are melted; stir until smooth.

Pour over crust. Sprinkle with remaining chips. Bake at 350° for 10-12 minutes or until chips are melted. Cool. **Yield:** about 4 dozen.

*Editor's Note: This recipe was tested in a 1,100-watt microwave.*

## Brownie Mounds

Mary Turner, Blountville, Tennessee

If you crave brownies but not the long baking time, try these quick chocolaty morsels. I usually make them for the holidays, but they're good any time of year.

    1/3    cup butter, softened
    3/4    cup sugar
    1/3    cup light corn syrup
      1    egg
      3    squares (1 ounce *each*) unsweetened
           chocolate, melted
      1    teaspoon vanilla extract
  1-2/3    cups all-purpose flour
    1/2    teaspoon baking powder
    1/4    teaspoon salt
    1/2    cup chopped walnuts

In a large mixing bowl, cream butter and sugar until light and fluffy. Add corn syrup and egg; beat well. Stir in chocolate and vanilla. Combine the flour, baking powder and salt; add to chocolate mixture. Beat well. Stir in walnuts.

Drop by tablespoonfuls 2 in. apart onto greased baking sheets. Bake at 350° for 10-12 minutes or until edges are firm. Remove to wire racks to cool. **Yield:** 3 dozen.

brownie cups

## Brownie Cups

Merrill Powers, Spearville, Kansas

This recipe for individual brownie cupcakes studded with pecan pieces is delicious. The crinkly tops of these chewy treats are so pretty that they don't need frosting.

    1   cup butter
    1   cup (6 ounces) semisweet chocolate chips
    1   cup chopped pecans
    4   eggs
1-1/2   cups sugar
    1   cup all-purpose flour
    1   teaspoon vanilla extract

In a small saucepan over low heat, melt the butter and chocolate chips, stirring until smooth. Cool. Add pecans; stir until well-coated. In a large bowl, combine the eggs, sugar, flour and vanilla. Fold in chocolate mixture.

Fill paper-lined muffin cups two-thirds full. Bake at 325° for 35-38 minutes or until a toothpick inserted near the center comes out clean. Remove from pans to wire racks to cool. **Yield:** about 1-1/2 dozen.

## Favorite Cake Brownies

Margaret Harris, Edgecomb, Maine

If you prefer cake-like brownies instead of the fudgy sort, you'll adore this from-scratch recipe. Topped with confectioners' sugar and a chocolate drizzle, they can't be beat.

    1/4   cup butter
    2/3   cup sugar
    1/4   cup baking cocoa
      1   egg white
    1/3   cup milk
    1/2   teaspoon vanilla extract
    3/4   cup all-purpose flour
    1/4   teaspoon baking powder
    1/4   teaspoon baking soda
    1/3   cup chopped nuts
      1   teaspoon confectioners' sugar
TOPPING:
    1/2   cup confectioners' sugar
      1   tablespoon baking cocoa
      1   tablespoon milk
    1/4   teaspoon vanilla extract

In a large saucepan, melt butter; remove from the heat. Stir in sugar and cocoa until smooth. Add the egg white, milk and vanilla; stir just until blended. Combine flour, baking powder and baking soda; stir into chocolate mixture just until blended. Stir in nuts.

Pour into a 9-in. square baking pan coated with nonstick cooking spray. Bake at 350° for 16-18 minutes or until a toothpick inserted near the center comes out clean. Cool on a wire rack. Dust brownies with confectioners' sugar.

In a small bowl, combine topping ingredients until smooth. Drizzle over brownies. **Yield:** 16 brownies.

## Chocolate Toffee Crunchies

Joni Crans, Woodhull, New York

From the buttery crust to the golden toffee, melted chocolate and chopped pecans, these sensational snacks are filled with unbeatable flavor.

    2   cups vanilla wafer crumbs
    1/4   cup packed brown sugar
    1/2   cup butter, melted
TOPPING:
    1/2   cup butter
    1/2   cup packed brown sugar
      1   cup (6 ounces) semisweet chocolate chips
    1/2   cup finely chopped pecans

In a small bowl, combine the crumbs, brown sugar and butter. Press into an ungreased 13-in. x 9-in. x 2-in. baking pan. Bake at 350° for 8-10 minutes or until lightly browned.

In a small saucepan, bring butter and brown sugar to a boil over medium heat; boil and stir for 1 minute. Pour evenly over crust.

Bake at 350° for 10 minutes. Remove from oven; let stand for 2 minutes. Sprinkle with chocolate chips; let stand until chocolate is melted. Spread evenly over top; sprinkle with pecans. Cool completely before cutting. **Yield:** 4 dozen.

chocolate toffee crunchies

candy bar brownies

## Candy Bar Brownies
Sharon Evans, Rockwell, Iowa

Two kinds of chocolate candy bars baked into these brownies make them an extra-special treat.

```
3/4    cup butter, melted
  2    cups sugar
  4    eggs
  2    teaspoons vanilla extract
1-1/2  cups all-purpose flour
  1/3  cup baking cocoa
  1/2  teaspoon baking powder
  1/4  teaspoon salt
  4    Snickers bars (2.07 ounces each), cut into
       1/4-inch pieces
  3    plain milk chocolate candy bars (1.55 ounces
       each), coarsely chopped
```

In a large bowl, combine the butter, sugar, eggs and vanilla. In a small bowl, combine flour, cocoa, baking powder and salt; set aside 1/4 cup. Stir remaining dry ingredients into the egg mixture until well combined. Toss Snickers pieces with reserved flour mixture; stir into batter.

Transfer to a greased 13-in. x 9-in. x 2-in. baking pan. Sprinkle with milk chocolate candy bar pieces. Bake at 350° for 30-35 minutes or until a toothpick inserted near the center comes out clean (do not overbake). Cool on a wire rack. Chill before cutting. **Yield:** 3 dozen.

## Chocolate Bliss Brownies
Juanita Lou Williams, Enid, Oklahoma

I first tried these at a brunch and begged the hostess for the recipe. Sometimes I'll eliminate the frosting and just sprinkle the top with confectioners' sugar.

```
1/2  cup butter, softened
  1  cup sugar
  4  eggs
  1  can (16 ounces) chocolate syrup
  1  cup all-purpose flour
  1  cup chopped nuts
  1  teaspoon salt
```
FROSTING:
```
  6  tablespoons butter, cubed
```

```
1-1/2  cups sugar
  1/3  cup milk
  1/2  cup semisweet chocolate chips
```

In a large mixing bowl, cream the butter and sugar. Add eggs, one at a time, beating well after each addition. Add chocolate syrup. Beat in flour, nuts and salt until blended.

Pour into a greased 13-in. x 9-in. x 2-in. baking pan. Bake at 350° for 25-30 minutes or until a toothpick inserted near the center comes out clean (brownies may appear moist). Cool on a wire rack.

In a small saucepan, melt butter. Add sugar and milk. Bring to a boil; boil for 30 seconds. Remove from the heat; stir in the chips until melted. Beat until frosting reaches spreading consistency. Frost cooled brownies; cut. **Yield:** 4-1/2 dozen.

## Feeding-Time Snack Bars
Ame Andrews, Little Rock, Arkansas

I assured my friend that she didn't have to wait to try one of these scrumptious brownies until she got up in the middle of the night to feed the baby! But the chocolaty treats are a perfect anytime pick-me-up for new parents who are short on sleep and energy.

```
1-1/3  cups all-purpose flour
1-1/4  cups sugar
  1/2  cup baking cocoa
    1  teaspoon baking powder
  1/2  teaspoon salt
    4  eggs, lightly beaten
  3/4  cup butter, melted
  1/2  cup each milk chocolate chips, semisweet
       chocolate chips and vanilla or white chips
    3  Snickers candy bars (2.07 ounces each), cut
       into 1/4-inch pieces
```

In a large bowl, combine the flour, sugar, cocoa, baking powder and salt. Combine the eggs and butter; add to the dry ingredients and mix well. Stir in chips.

Transfer to a greased 13-in. x 9-in. x 2-in. baking pan. Bake at 350° for 25-30 minutes or until a toothpick inserted near the center comes out clean. Immediately sprinkle with candy bar pieces. Cool on a wire rack. Cut into bars. **Yield:** 2 dozen.

feeding-time snack bars

# Chapter 3

p. 42

p. 41

p. 43

p. 46

p. 51

# Fruit-Filled Snacks

Mix up the pace with these fruity baked treats. The brownies and bars offered here will dazzle your taste buds with fresh berry, zesty lemon, tangy orange and other tantalizing flavors.

raspberry nut bars

## Raspberry Nut Bars

Beth Ask, Ulster, Pennsylvania

Raspberry jam makes it a snap to whip up these down-home treats. Each bite is loaded with comforting flavor.

3/4 cup butter, softened
1/3 cup packed brown sugar
1/4 cup sugar
1 egg
1 teaspoon vanilla extract
2 cups all-purpose flour
1 teaspoon baking powder
1/4 teaspoon baking soda
1/4 teaspoon salt
3/4 cup chopped pecans, *divided*
2/3 cup raspberry jam
2 tablespoons lemon juice
GLAZE:
1/2 cup confectioners' sugar
2 teaspoons milk

In a large mixing bowl, cream butter and sugars. Beat in egg and vanilla. Combine the flour, baking powder, baking soda and salt; add to creamed mixture. Stir in 1/2 cup pecans.

Spread half of the dough into a greased 13-in. x 9-in. x 2-in. baking pan. Combine jam and lemon juice until blended; spread over dough. Dollop remaining dough over top. Sprinkle with remaining pecans.

Bake at 325° for 30-35 minutes or until lightly browned. Cool. Combine glaze ingredients; drizzle over bars. **Yield:** 3 dozen.

## Lime Coconut Bars

Mary Jane Jones, Williamstown, West Virginia

I found this dessert among my mother's recipe collection. I sometimes garnish the tangy bars with whipped topping and wedges of lime.

3/4 cup finely crushed crisp sugar cookies
3 tablespoons butter
2-1/4 cups flaked coconut
FILLING:
1/4 cup butter, softened
3/4 cup sugar
1/2 cup lime juice
4-1/2 teaspoons yellow cornmeal
Pinch salt
4 egg yolks
1 teaspoon grated lime peel
Confectioners' sugar

Place the crushed cookies in a bowl. Cut in butter until mixture resembles coarse crumbs. Stir in coconut; set aside 1 cup for topping. Press the remaining mixture into a greased 8-in. baking dish. Bake at 350° for 13-15 minutes or until golden brown.

Meanwhile, for filling, combine the butter, sugar, lime juice, cornmeal and salt in a heavy saucepan. Cook and stir over low heat until sugar is dissolved and cornmeal is softened, about 10 minutes. Remove from the heat.

In a small bowl, lightly beat the egg yolks. Stir a small amount of hot lime mixture into the yolks; return all to the pan, stirring constantly. Cook and stir until a thermometer reads 160° and mixture coats the back of a metal spoon, about 20 minutes. Remove from the heat; stir in lime peel. Pour over the crust; sprinkle with reserved coconut mixture. Bake at 350° for 18-20 minutes or until golden brown. Cool completely on a wire rack. Dust with confectioners' sugar. **Yield:** 16 bars.

*Editor's Note: The cornmeal is used as a thickener in the filling.*

lime coconut bars

date bar dessert

## Date Bar Dessert

Jill McCon, Montrose, Michigan

My mother copied this recipe from a Quaker Oats box in the 1950s, and it remains one of our most loved treats today. I serve the date-filled squares as a snack or for a dessert topped with a dollop of whipped cream.

```
1-3/4   cups old-fashioned oats
1-1/2   cups all-purpose flour
    1   cup packed brown sugar
    1   teaspoon baking soda
  1/2   teaspoon salt
    1   cup cold butter, cubed
2-1/2   cups chopped dates
  3/4   cup sugar
  3/4   cup water
  1/2   cup chopped walnuts
Whipped topping
```

In a large bowl, combine the oats, flour, brown sugar, baking soda and salt. Cut in butter until mixture resembles coarse crumbs. Press into a greased 13-in. x 9-in. x 2-in. baking pan.

In a large saucepan, combine the dates, sugar and water. Cook for 10 minutes or until thickened, stirring frequently. Stir in walnuts. Spread over crust.

Bake at 350° for 30 minutes. Cool on a wire rack. Cut into squares; top with whipped topping. **Yield:** 18 servings.

## Apricot Oat Bars

Dorothy Myrick, Kent, Washington

With an oat-filled crust and golden crumb topping, these apricot-filled bars are sweet and chewy. Snackers can't resist the fruity bites.

```
    1   cup quick-cooking oats
    1   cup all-purpose flour
  2/3   cup packed brown sugar
```

```
  1/4   teaspoon baking soda
  1/4   teaspoon salt
  1/4   cup canola oil
    3   tablespoons unsweetened apple juice
    1   jar (10 ounces) apricot spreadable fruit
```

In a large bowl, combine the oats, flour, brown sugar, baking soda and salt. Add oil and apple juice; stir until moistened. Set aside 1/2 cup for topping.

Press remaining oat mixture into an 11-in. x 7-in. x 2-in. baking pan coated with nonstick cooking spray. Spread the apricot fruit spread to within 1/4 in. of edges. Sprinkle with reserved oat mixture. Bake at 325° for 30-35 minutes or until golden brown. **Yield:** 16 bars.

## Raspberry Crunch Brownies

Rita Winter Berger, Hudson, Montana

These rich brownies, with dark chocolate flavor and nut-like crunch, prove that desserts don't have to be full of fat to be splendid.

```
  1/4   cup vegetable oil
1-1/4   cups sugar
    4   egg whites
    1   cup all-purpose flour
  2/3   cup baking cocoa
  1/2   teaspoon baking powder
  1/4   teaspoon salt
1-1/2   teaspoons vanilla extract
Nonstick vegetable spray
  1/4   cup raspberry jam
    2   tablespoons Grape-Nuts cereal, optional
```

In a large mixing bowl, beat oil and sugar until blended. Beat in egg whites. Combine the flour, cocoa, baking powder and salt; gradually add to sugar mixture just until moistened. Stir in vanilla. (Batter will be thick.)

Coat a 9-in. square pan with vegetable spray. Spread batter into pan. Bake at 350° for 20 to 25 minutes or until a toothpick inserted in the center comes out clean. Cool 10 minutes on a wire rack. Spread with jam and sprinkle with Grape-Nuts if desired. Cool completely. **Yield:** 2 dozen.

# Brownie Point

If the edges of your brownies are coming out too hard, it may be the baking pan you're using. Dark-colored pans can often cause the edges of baked goods to brown quicker than the rest of the item.

## Cranberry-Orange Bars

Margaret Adelman, Bellingham, Minnesota

My mother has had this recipe for years. I love it! These bars make great snacks, but they can also be served for a nice dessert.

- 3 cups fresh *or* frozen cranberries
- 2 large unpeeled oranges, cut into quarters and seeded
- 2-1/2 cups sugar
- 3 tablespoons cornstarch
- 1 teaspoon ground ginger
- 1/2 cup chopped nuts, optional

CRUST:
- 3-1/4 cups all-purpose flour
- 3/4 cup sugar
- 1 tablespoon grated lemon peel
- 1 cup butter, cubed
- 3 egg yolks
- 3/4 teaspoon vanilla extract
- 1 to 2 tablespoons water

Grind cranberries and oranges (including peel). Set aside. In a large saucepan, combine the sugar, cornstarch and ginger. Add ground fruit; bring to a boil. Reduce heat; cook and stir for 15 minutes or until thickened. Remove from the heat; stir in the nuts if desired. Set aside to cool.

Meanwhile, for crust, in a large bowl, combine the flour, sugar and lemon peel. Cut in butter until coarse crumbs form. Add egg yolks and vanilla. Gradually add water, tossing with a fork until dough forms a ball.

Pat two-thirds of dough into a greased 13-in. x 9-in. x 2-in. baking pan. Cover with cranberry-orange mixture. Crumble remaining dough on top. Bake at 425° for 20-25 minutes or until topping is golden brown. Cool on a wire rack; cut into bars. **Yield:** about 2-1/2 dozen.

berries 'n cream brownies

## Berries 'n Cream Brownies

Anna Lapp, New Holland, Pennsylvania

If you like chocolate-covered strawberries, you'll adore this idea. A fudgy brownie, whipped topping and fresh fruit make it a no-fuss feast for the eyes as well as the taste buds. It's a smart summer dessert.

- 1 package fudge brownie mix (13-inch x 9-inch pan size)
- 1 carton (8 ounces) frozen whipped topping, thawed
- 4 cups quartered fresh strawberries
- 1/3 cup chocolate hard-shell ice cream topping

Prepare and bake brownies according to package directions, using a greased 13-in. x 9-in. x 2-in. baking pan. Cool completely on a wire rack.

Spread whipped topping over brownies. Arrange strawberries cut side down over top. Drizzle with chocolate topping. Refrigerate for at least 30 minutes before serving. **Yield:** 12-15 servings.

# Brownie Point

Clear plastic wrap is perfect for wrapping individual fruit bars. Cut a roll of the wrap in half, and you'll have two narrow rolls instead of one wide roll. You'll find that the smaller rolls come in handy for wrapping lunchbox treats and other sweet surprises.

cranberry-orange bars

## Coconut Raspberry Bars

Amanda Denton, Barre, Vermont

While mixing a batch of plain bars, I was inspired to add raspberry preserves and flaked coconut to the dough…and wound up with these yummy treats that are now a family staple. They're a great change from chocolate brownies.

layered coconut bars

| | |
|---|---|
| 3/4 | cup butter, softened |
| 1 | cup sugar |
| 1 | egg |
| 1/2 | teaspoon vanilla extract |
| 2 | cups all-purpose flour |
| 1/4 | teaspoon baking powder |
| 2 | cups flaked coconut, *divided* |
| 1/2 | cup chopped walnuts |
| 1 | jar (12 ounces) raspberry preserves |
| 1 | cup vanilla *or* white chips |

In a large mixing bowl, cream butter and sugar until light and fluffy. Beat in egg and vanilla. Combine flour and baking powder; gradually add to the creamed mixture. Stir in 1-1/4 cups coconut and the walnuts.

Press three-fourths of the dough into a greased 13-in. x 9-in. x 2-in. baking pan. Spread with preserves. Sprinkle with chips and remaining coconut. Crumble remaining dough over the top; press lightly. Bake at 350° for 30-35 minutes or until golden brown. Cool on a wire rack. Cut into squares. **Yield:** 3 dozen.

## Lemon Graham Squares

Janis Plourde, Smooth Rock Falls, Ontario

My Aunt Jackie brought these lemon bars to every family gathering. They're my favorite lemon dessert. The crispy top and bottom offer a perfect texture.

| | |
|---|---|
| 1 | can (14 ounces) sweetened condensed milk |
| 1/2 | cup lemon juice |
| 1-1/2 | cups graham cracker crumbs (about 24 squares) |
| 3/4 | cup all-purpose flour |
| 1/3 | cup packed brown sugar |
| 1/2 | teaspoon baking powder |
| Pinch salt | |
| 1/2 | cup butter, melted |

In a small bowl, combine the milk and lemon juice; set aside. In a large bowl, combine the cracker crumbs, flour, brown sugar, baking powder and salt. Stir in butter until crumbly.

Press half of the crumb mixture into a greased 9-in. square baking dish. Pour lemon mixture over crust; sprinkle with remaining crumbs. Bake at 375° for 20-25 minutes or until lightly browned. Cool on a wire rack. **Yield:** 3 dozen.

## Layered Coconut Bars

Patty Bryant, Cedar Knolls, New Jersey

Folks will save room for dessert when these bars are part of the menu. They're chock-full of fun ingredients such as coconut and walnuts.

| | |
|---|---|
| 1/4 | cup butter, melted |
| 1 | cup vanilla wafer crumbs |
| 1/2 | cup semisweet chocolate chips |
| 1/4 | cup chopped walnuts |
| 3/4 | cup flaked coconut |
| 2/3 | cup sweetened condensed milk |
| Candied fruit, optional | |

In a small bowl, combine butter and crumbs until crumbly. Press into an ungreased 8-in. square baking dish. Sprinkle with chocolate chips, walnuts and coconut. Pour milk over all. Bake at 350° for 25 minutes. Decorate with candied fruit if desired. **Yield:** 9 servings.

lemon graham squares

lemon cheesecake squares

## Lemon Cheesecake Squares

Peggy Reddick, Cumming, Georgia

Whether I'm hosting friends or sending a plate to work with my husband, these creamy, elegant cheesecake squares are always a hit. It's a wonderful make-ahead dessert that easily serves a large group.

|       |                               |
| ----- | ----------------------------- |
| 3/4   | cup shortening                |
| 1/3   | cup packed brown sugar        |
| 1-1/4 | cups all-purpose flour        |
| 1     | cup rolled oats               |
| 1/4   | teaspoon salt                 |
| 1/2   | cup seedless raspberry jam    |

FILLING:
|       |                                          |
| ----- | ---------------------------------------- |
| 4     | packages (8 ounces *each*) cream cheese, softened |
| 1-1/2 | cups sugar                               |
| 1/4   | cup all-purpose flour                    |
| 4     | eggs                                     |
| 1/3   | cup lemon juice                          |
| 4     | teaspoons grated lemon peel              |

In a large mixing bowl, cream shortening and brown sugar until light and fluffy. Combine the flour, oats and salt; gradually add to creamed mixture.

Press dough into a greased 13-in. x 9-in. x 2-in. baking dish. Bake at 350° for 15-18 minutes or until golden brown. Spread with jam.

For filling, in a large mixing bowl, beat the cream cheese, sugar and flour until smooth. Beat in the eggs, lemon juice and peel just until blended. Carefully spoon over jam.

Bake at 350° for 30-35 minutes or until center is almost set. Cool on a wire rack. Cover and store in the refrigerator. **Yield:** 20 servings.

## Blueberry Oat Bars

Deena Hubler, Jasper, Indiana

Oats add plenty of crunch to the tasty crust and crumbly topping of these fruity specialties. I often bake the blueberry bites for church parties and other get-togethers, and they always go over well.

|       |                                    |
| ----- | ---------------------------------- |
| 1-1/2 | cups all-purpose flour             |
| 1-1/2 | cups quick-cooking oats            |
| 1-1/2 | cups sugar, *divided*              |
| 1/2   | teaspoon baking soda               |
| 3/4   | cup cold butter                    |
| 2     | cups fresh *or* frozen blueberries |
| 2     | tablespoons cornstarch             |
| 2     | tablespoons lemon juice            |

In a large bowl, combine the flour, oats, 1 cup sugar and baking soda. Cut in butter until mixture resembles coarse crumbs. Reserve 2 cups for topping. Press remaining crumb mixture into a greased 13-in. x 9-in. x 2-in. baking pan; set aside.

In a large saucepan, combine blueberries, cornstarch, lemon juice and remaining sugar. Bring to a boil; boil for 2 minutes, stirring constantly.

Spread evenly over the crust. Sprinkle with the reserved crumb mixture.

Bake at 375° for 25 minutes or until lightly browned. Cool on a wire rack. Cut into bars. **Yield:** 2-1/2 to 3 dozen.

## Chocolate Lemon Cream Bars

Renee Schwebach, Dumont, Minnesota

A jazzed-up chocolate cake mix forms the layers that sandwich a lemony cream cheese center in these goodies. I took the bars to the office, and they were a success with my co-workers.

|     |                                        |
| --- | -------------------------------------- |
| 1   | package (18-1/4 ounces) devil's food cake mix |
| 1/2 | cup butter, softened                   |
| 1   | egg                                    |
| 1/2 | cup chopped walnuts                    |

FILLING:
|     |                                          |
| --- | ---------------------------------------- |
| 1   | package (8 ounces) cream cheese, softened |
| 1   | can (14 ounces) sweetened condensed milk |
| 1   | egg                                      |
| 3   | tablespoons lemon juice                  |
| 2   | to 3 teaspoons grated lemon peel         |

In a large mixing bowl, beat the cake mix, butter and egg on low speed until combined. Stir in walnuts. Set aside 1 cup for topping. Press the remaining mixture into a greased 13-in. x 9-in. x 2-in. baking pan. Bake at 350° for 8-10 minutes or until set. Cool for 5 minutes.

In a large mixing bowl, beat cream cheese until smooth. Beat in the milk, egg, lemon juice and peel. Pour over the crust. Crumble reserved cake mixture over the top.

Bake for 18-22 minutes or until set. Cool completely before cutting. Store in the refrigerator. **Yield:** 4 dozen.

raspberry citrus bars

## Raspberry Citrus Bars

Ruby Nelson, Mountain Home, Arkansas

Here's a treat that was an instant hit with my family when I first made it. The combination of raspberries, lemon juice and orange peel gives it a refreshing flavor.

    1   cup butter, softened
  3/4   cup confectioners' sugar
2-1/4   cups all-purpose flour, divided
    4   eggs
1-1/2   cups sugar
  1/3   cup lemon juice
    2   tablespoons grated orange peel
    1   teaspoon baking powder
1-1/2   cups unsweetened raspberries

In a large mixing bowl, cream butter and confectioners' sugar until light and fluffy. Gradually add 2 cups flour just until combined.

Press mixture into a greased 13-in. x 9-in. x 2-in. baking pan. Bake at 350° for 20 minutes or until lightly browned.

Meanwhile, in a large mixing bowl, beat the eggs, sugar, lemon juice and orange peel. Combine the baking powder and remaining flour; gradually add to egg mixture. Sprinkle raspberries over the crust. Pour filling over the berries.

Bake for 30-35 minutes or until lightly browned and filing is set. Cool on a wire rack. Store in the refrigerator. **Yield:** 12-15 servings.

## Granola Fruit Bars

Kim Finup, Kalamazoo, Michigan

We prefer these chewy wholesome treats to store-bought granola bars. They combine apple and peanut butter and make a great grab-and-go breakfast or an anytime snack.

  1/2   cup chopped dried apples
  1/3   cup honey
  1/4   cup raisins
    1   tablespoon brown sugar
  1/3   cup peanut butter

  1/4   cup apple butter
  1/2   teaspoon ground cinnamon
  1/2   cup old-fashioned oats
  1/3   cup honey crunch or toasted wheat germ
  1/4   cup chopped pecans
2-1/2   cups cornflakes

In a large saucepan, combine the apples, honey, raisins and brown sugar. Bring to a boil over medium heat, stirring often. Cook and stir 1 minute longer. Remove from the heat; stir in peanut butter until melted.

Add apple butter and cinnamon. Stir in the oats, wheat germ and pecans. Fold in cornflakes. Press firmly into an 8-in. square pan coated with nonstick cooking spray. Refrigerate for 1 hour or until set. Cut into bars. Store in an airtight container in the refrigerator. **Yield:** 8 servings.

*Editor's Note:* This recipe was tested with commercially prepared apple butter.

## Grandma's Date Bars

Marilyn Reid, Cherry Creek, New York

These nicely textured bars are delicious. My great-grandmother, who was born in 1868, made these bars, and the recipe has come down through the generations. Now my children are baking them.

    1   cup sugar
    1   cup all-purpose flour
    1   teaspoon baking powder
  1/2   teaspoon salt
    1   cup chopped dates
    1   cup chopped walnuts
    3   eggs, beaten
Confectioners' sugar

In a large bowl, combine the first seven ingredients. Transfer to a greased 8-in. square baking pan.

Bake at 350° for 25 minutes or until a toothpick inserted near the center comes out clean. Cool on a wire rack. Dust with confectioners' sugar. Cut into squares. **Yield:** 16 servings.

grandma's date bars

## Banana-Berry Brownie Pizza
Tina Jacobs, Wantage, New Jersey

I like to make this dessert in June and early July so I can use fresh strawberries. The fruit lightens up the rich chocolate flavor and pleases everyone.

| | |
|---|---|
| 1 | package fudge brownie mix (13-inch x 9-inch size) |
| 1/3 | cup boiling water |
| 1/4 | cup vegetable oil |
| 1 | egg |

TOPPING:

| | |
|---|---|
| 1 | package (8 ounces) cream cheese, softened |
| 1/4 | cup sugar |
| 1 | egg |
| 1 | teaspoon vanilla extract |
| 2 | cups sliced fresh strawberries |
| 1 | to 2 medium firm bananas, sliced |
| 1 | square (1 ounce) semisweet chocolate, melted |

In a large bowl, combine the brownie mix, water, oil and egg until well blended. Spread into a greased and floured 12-in. pizza pan. Bake at 350° for 25 minutes.

In a large mixing bowl, beat the cream cheese, sugar, egg and vanilla until smooth. Spread over brownie crust. Bake 15 minutes longer or until topping is set. Cool on a wire rack.

Just before serving, arrange strawberries and bananas over topping; drizzle with chocolate. Refrigerate leftovers. **Yield:** 10-12 servings.

banana-berry brownie pizza

peaches 'n cream bars

## Peaches 'n Cream Bars
Hubert Scott, Cockeysville, Maryland

If you like peach pie, you'll love these easy-to-make bars with a crunchy almond topping.

| | |
|---|---|
| 1 | tube (8 ounces) refrigerated crescent rolls |
| 1 | package (8 ounces) cream cheese, softened |
| 1/2 | cup sugar |
| 1/4 | teaspoon almond extract |
| 1 | can (21 ounces) peach pie filling |
| 1/2 | cup all-purpose flour |
| 1/4 | cup packed brown sugar |
| 3 | tablespoons cold butter |
| 1/2 | cup sliced almonds |

Unroll crescent dough into one long rectangle. Press onto the bottom and slightly up the sides of a greased 13-in. x 9-in. x 2-in. baking pan; seal perforations. Bake at 375° for 5 minutes. Cool completely on a wire rack.

In a large mixing bowl, beat the cream cheese, sugar and extract until smooth. Spread over crust. Spoon pie filling over cream cheese layer. In a small bowl, combine flour and brown sugar. Cut in butter until mixture resembles coarse crumbs. Stir in nuts; sprinkle over peach filling.

Bake at 375° for 25-28 minutes or until edges are golden brown. Cool for 1 hour on a wire rack. Store in the refrigerator. **Yield:** about 2 dozen.

## Rhubarb Dream Bars
Marion Tomlinson, Madison, Wisconsin

Looking for a different way to use rhubarb? I top a tender shortbread-like crust with rhubarb, walnuts and coconut with delicious results.

| | |
|---|---|
| 1-1/4 | cups all-purpose flour, *divided* |
| 1/3 | cup confectioners' sugar |
| 1/2 | cup cold butter, cubed |
| 1-1/4 | to 1-1/2 cups sugar |
| 2 | eggs |
| 2 | cups diced fresh *or* frozen rhubarb |

1/2　cup chopped walnuts
1/2　cup flaked coconut

In a large bowl, combine 1 cup flour and confectioners' sugar. Cut in the butter until crumbly. Pat into a lightly greased 13-in. x 9-in. x 2-in. baking dish. Bake at 350° for 13-15 minutes or until edges are lightly browned.

In a large bowl, combine sugar and remaining flour. Add eggs. Stir in the rhubarb, walnuts and coconut; pour over crust. Bake 30-35 minutes longer or until set. Cool on a wire rack. Cut into bars. **Yield:** 2-1/2 to 3 dozen.

*Editor's Note: If using frozen rhubarb, measure rhubarb while still frozen, then thaw completely. Drain in a colander, but do not press liquid out.*

## Coconut Cranberry Bars

Dolly McDonald, Edmonton, Alberta

I begged a neighbor for her recipe after tasting these yummy bars at a coffee she hosted. The colors from the cranberries and white chips make them real eye-pleasers!

1-1/2　cups graham cracker crumbs (about 24 squares)
1/2　cup butter, melted
1-1/2　cups vanilla *or* white chips
1-1/2　cups dried cranberries
1　can (14 ounces) sweetened condensed milk
1　cup flaked coconut
1　cup pecan halves

In a small bowl, combine cracker crumbs and butter until crumbly; press into a greased 13-in. x 9-in. x 2-in. baking pan. In a large bowl, combine the remaining ingredients.

Gently spread over crust. Bake at 350° for 25-28 minutes or until edges are golden brown. Cool on a wire rack. Cut into bars. **Yield:** 3 dozen.

coconut cranberry bars

blueberry lattice bars

## Blueberry Lattice Bars

Debbie Ayers, Baileyville, Maine

Since our area has an annual blueberry festival, my daughters and I are always looking for great new berry recipes to enter in the cooking contest. These lovely bars won a blue ribbon one year.

1　cup butter, softened
1/2　cup sugar
1　egg
2-3/4　cups all-purpose flour
1/2　teaspoon vanilla extract
1/4　teaspoon salt
FILLING:
3　cups fresh *or* frozen blueberries
1　cup sugar
3　tablespoons cornstarch

In a large mixing bowl, cream butter and sugar. Add the egg, flour, vanilla and salt. Cover and refrigerate for 2 hours.

Meanwhile, in a small saucepan, bring the blueberries, sugar and cornstarch to a boil. Cook and stir for 2 minutes or until thickened.

Roll two-thirds of the dough into a 14-in. x 10-in. rectangle. Place in a greased 13-in. x 9-in. x 2-in. baking dish. Top with filling. Roll out remaining dough to 1/4-in. thickness. Cut into 1/2-in.-wide strips; make a lattice crust over filling.

Bake at 375° for 30-35 minutes or until top is golden brown. Cool on a wire rack. Cut into bars. **Yield:** 2 dozen.

cherry streusel bars

## Cherry Streusel Bars

Ellen Borst, Park Falls, Wisconsin

I combined my grandmother's apple crisp topping with a traditional cherry pie recipe to come up with these fun and flavorful bars.

    4    cups all-purpose flour, *divided*
    2    teaspoons sugar
    1    teaspoon salt
    3/4  cup butter-flavored shortening
    1    egg
    1/4  cup water
    1-1/2 teaspoons cider vinegar
    2    cans (21 ounces *each*) cherry pie filling
    1    tablespoon grated orange peel
    1-1/4 cups packed brown sugar
    1/2  teaspoon ground cinnamon
    1    cup cold butter, cubed

In a large bowl, combine 2 cups flour, sugar and salt; cut in shortening until crumbly. In another bowl, whisk the egg, water and vinegar. Stir into flour mixture with a fork until a soft ball forms.

On a lightly floured surface, roll out dough into a 15-in. x 10-in. rectangle. Transfer to a greased 15-in. x 10-in. x 1-in. baking pan. Bake at 400° for 6-8 minutes or until firm and dry to the touch.

Meanwhile, combine pie filling and orange peel; set aside. In a large bowl, combine the brown sugar, cinnamon and remaining flour; cut in butter until crumbly.

Spread cherry mixture over crust. Sprinkle with crumb mixture. Bake at 400° for 20-25 minutes or until golden brown. Cool on a wire rack for 20 minutes before cutting. **Yield:** about 2-1/2 dozen.

## Fruitcake Squares

Nora Seaton, McLean, Virginia

My family prefers these scrumptious squares to the larger, more traditional fruitcake. Since the treats are so quick and simple to make, I always include several batches in my annual holiday baking spree.

    6    tablespoons butter, melted
    4    cups crushed vanilla wafers
    1    cup pecan halves
    3/4  cup chopped dates
    3/4  cup chopped mixed candied fruit
    1/2  cup chopped candied pineapple
    1    can (14 ounces) sweetened condensed milk
    1    teaspoon vanilla extract

Pour butter into a 15-in. x 10-in. x 1-in. baking pan. Sprinkle with wafer crumbs. Arrange pecans and fruit over crumbs; press down gently. Combine milk and vanilla; pour evenly over fruit. Bake at 350° for 20-25 minutes or until lightly browned. Cool on a wire rack. **Yield:** about 3 dozen.

## Apricot-Coconut Bars

Helen Cluts, Sioux Falls, South Dakota

My family likes snacking on these rich-tasting fruit bars. The recipe is one I've used and shared for over 30 years.

    1    cup all-purpose flour
    1    teaspoon baking powder
    1/2  cup butter
    1    egg
    1    tablespoon milk
    1    cup apricot preserves
TOPPING:
    1    egg, lightly beaten
    2/3  cup sugar
    1/4  cup butter, melted
    1    teaspoon vanilla extract
    2    cups flaked coconut

In a large bowl, combine flour and baking powder. Cut in butter until the mixture resembles coarse crumbs. Beat the egg and milk; stir into flour mixture.

Spread in a greased 9-in. square baking pan. Spread preserves over crust. Combine topping ingredients; carefully drop by tablespoonfuls over apricot layer. Bake at 350° for 25-30 minutes or until golden brown. Cool on a wire rack; cut into small bars. **Yield:** 2 to 2-1/2 dozen.

apricot-coconut bars

pineapple coconut squares

## Pineapple Coconut Squares

Elaine Anderson, New Galilee, Pennsylvania

I don't remember where I got this recipe, but I'm sure glad I have it. The tangy pineapple and flaked coconut give these bars an unbeatable, tropical flair.

2 tablespoons butter, melted
3 tablespoons sugar
1 egg
1 cup all-purpose flour
1 teaspoon baking powder
2 cans (8 ounces *each*) unsweetened crushed pineapple, drained
TOPPING:
1 tablespoon butter, melted
1 cup sugar
2 eggs
2 cups flaked coconut

In a large mixing bowl, cream butter and sugar until light and fluffy. Beat in egg. Combine flour and baking powder; stir into creamed mixture. Press into a 9-in. square baking dish coated with nonstick cooking spray. Spread pineapple over crust; set aside.

For topping, in a small mixing bowl, beat butter and sugar until blended. Beat in eggs. Stir in coconut. Spread over pineapple. Bake at 325° for 35-40 minutes or until golden brown. Cool on a wire rack before cutting. **Yield:** 16 servings.

## Brownie Point

A bit of shredded zucchini added to a boxed brownie mix makes extra moist and tasty treats.

## Fruit Cocktail Bars

Linda Tackman, Escanaba, Michigan

My mother passed this recipe on to me. The moist bars have a delightful fruity taste, perfect for potlucks in both winter and spring.

1-1/2 cups sugar
2 eggs
1 can (15 ounces) fruit cocktail, undrained
1 teaspoon vanilla extract
2-1/4 cups all-purpose flour
1-1/2 teaspoons baking soda
1 teaspoon salt
1-1/3 cups flaked coconut
1 cup chopped walnuts
GLAZE:
1/2 cup sugar
1/4 cup butter, cubed
2 tablespoons milk
1/4 teaspoon vanilla extract

In a large mixing bowl, beat sugar and eggs until blended. Beat in fruit cocktail and vanilla. Combine the flour, baking soda and salt; add to the creamed mixture until well blended.

Pour into a greased 15-in. x 10-in. x 1-in. baking pan. Sprinkle with coconut and walnuts. Bake at 350° for 20-25 minutes or until a toothpick inserted near the center comes out clean. Cool on a rack for 10 minutes.

In a small saucepan, bring the sugar, butter and milk to a boil. Remove from the heat; stir in vanilla. Drizzle over cake. Cool. Cut into bars. **Yield:** 2-1/2 dozen.

fruit cocktail bars

## Cherry Bars

Jane Kamp, Grand Rapids, Michigan

Want something simple to satisfy a crowd? Try these festive, fruit-filled bars. With their pretty color from cherry pie filling and subtle almond flavor, they're destined to become one of your most requested goodies.

- 1   cup butter, softened
- 2   cups sugar
- 4   eggs
- 1   teaspoon vanilla extract
- 1/4 teaspoon almond extract
- 3   cups all-purpose flour
- 1   teaspoon salt
- 2   cans (21 ounces *each*) cherry pie filling

GLAZE:
- 1   cup confectioners' sugar
- 1/2 teaspoon vanilla extract
- 1/2 teaspoon almond extract
- 2   to 3 tablespoons milk

In a large mixing bowl, cream butter and sugar until light and fluffy. Add eggs, one at a time, beating well after each addition. Beat in the extracts. Combine the flour and the salt; gradually add to the creamed mixture just until combined.

Spread 3 cups batter into a greased 15-in. x 10-in. x 1-in. baking pan. Spread with pie filling. Drop the remaining batter by teaspoonfuls over filling.

Bake at 350° for 30-35 minutes or until a toothpick comes out clean. Cool on a wire rack. Combine the glaze ingredients; drizzle over bars. **Yield:** 5 dozen.

cherry bars

chocolate date squares

## Chocolate Date Squares

Pat Walter, Pine Island, Minnesota

My mother-in-law used to send these moist bars to my husband when he was in the Army. Once I received the recipe, they became a household staple.

- 2   cups chopped dates
- 1   cup hot water
- 1   cup sugar
- 2/3 cup shortening
- 2   eggs
- 1-1/2 cups all-purpose flour
- 1   teaspoon baking soda
- 1/2 teaspoon salt

TOPPING:
- 1   cup (6 ounces) semisweet chocolate chips
- 1/2 cup packed brown sugar
- 1/2 cup chopped nuts

In a small bowl, combine dates and water; set aside to cool (do not drain). In a large mixing bowl, cream sugar and shortening until light and fluffy. Beat in eggs. Combine the flour, baking soda and salt; gradually added to creamed mixture. Stir in dates.

Pour into a greased and floured 13-in. x 9-in. x 2-in. baking pan. Combine the topping ingredients; sprinkle over batter. Bake at 350° for 40 minutes or until a toothpick inserted near the center comes out clean. Cool on a wire rack. **Yield:** 24 servings.

## Glazed Persimmon Bars

Delores Leach, Penn Valley, California

For a tasty change of pace, give persimmon-flavored brownies a try. They are a wonderful way to take a break during the day.

- 1   cup mashed ripe persimmon pulp
- 1   cup sugar
- 1/2 cup vegetable oil
- 1   egg
- 1-1/2 teaspoons lemon juice
- 1-3/4 cups all-purpose flour
- 1   teaspoon baking soda

```
  1   teaspoon salt
  1   teaspoon ground cinnamon
  1   teaspoon ground nutmeg
 1/4  teaspoon ground cloves, optional
1-1/2 cups chopped dates or raisins
  1   cup chopped nuts
GLAZE:
  1   cup confectioners' sugar
  2   tablespoons lemon juice
```

In a large mixing bowl, combine the persimmon, sugar, oil, egg and lemon juice. Combine the flour, baking soda, salt and spices; add to sugar mixture. Stir in the dates and the nuts.

Spread into a greased 15-in. x 10-in. x 1-in. baking pan. Bake at 350° for 20-25 minutes or until a toothpick inserted near the center comes out clean. Cool in pan on a wire rack. Combine glaze ingredients; spread over bars. **Yield:** about 4 dozen.

## Peanut Jelly Bars

Sonja Blow, Reeds Spring, Missouri

A layer of grape jelly between a peanut-oatmeal crust and topping gives these bars the taste of a peanut butter and jelly sandwich. Kids of all ages love them!

```
 3/4  cup butter, softened
  1   cup packed brown sugar
1-1/2 cups all-purpose flour
  1   teaspoon salt
 1/2  teaspoon baking soda
1-1/2 cups quick-cooking oats
 1/2  cup chopped salted peanuts
  1   jar (12 ounces) grape jelly
```

In a large mixing bowl, cream butter and brown sugar. Combine the flour, salt and baking soda; gradually add to creamed mixture. Stir in oats and peanuts (mixture will be crumbly).

Press half of the mixture into a greased 13-in. x 9-in. baking pan. Spread with jelly. Cover with remaining crumb mixture. Bake at 400° for 25 minutes or until golden brown. Cool on a wire rack. Cut into bars. **Yield:** 2 dozen.

peanut jelly bars

raisin cinnamon bars

## Raisin Cinnamon Bars

Jean Morgan, Roscoe, Illinois

I've been making these simple iced bars for more than 40 years. They're easy to prepare for dessert or as a sweet treat with a cup of coffee.

```
 1/4  cup butter
  1   cup packed brown sugar
  1   egg
 1/2  cup hot brewed coffee
1-1/2 cups all-purpose flour
  1   teaspoon baking powder
 1/2  teaspoon ground cinnamon
 1/4  teaspoon baking soda
 1/4  teaspoon salt
 1/2  cup raisins
 1/4  cup chopped pecans
ICING:
  1   cup confectioners' sugar
 1/2  teaspoon vanilla extract
  4   to 5 teaspoons water
```

In a large mixing bowl, combine butter and brown sugar until crumbly, about 2 minutes. Beat in egg. Gradually beat in coffee. Combine the flour, baking powder, cinnamon, baking soda and salt. Gradually add to the coffee mixture until blended. Stir in raisins and pecans.

Transfer to a 13-in. x 9-in. x 2-in. baking pan coated with nonstick cooking spray. Bake at 350° for 18-20 minutes or until edges begin to pull away from the sides of the pan and a toothpick inserted near the center comes out clean. Cool on a wire rack for 5 minutes.

Meanwhile for icing, in a small bowl, combine the confectioners' sugar, vanilla and enough water to achieve spreading consistency. Spread over warm bars. **Yield:** 1-1/2 dozen.

raspberry brownies a la mode

## Raspberry Brownies a la Mode

Denise Elder, Hanover, Ontario

This fudgy recipe makes a lot, so it's perfect for parties. Guests will think you fussed over the raspberry sauce drizzled over each wedge, but it's easy to make. When I worked in a restaurant, I always prepared it for special-occasion menus.

        5    squares (1 ounce *each*) unsweetened
             chocolate, coarsely chopped
      2/3    cup butter (no substitutes)
        3    eggs
    2-3/4    cups sugar, *divided*
        2    teaspoons vanilla extract
        1    cup all-purpose flour
        1    cup (6 ounces) semisweet chocolate chips
        3    cups fresh raspberries
        1    tablespoon lemon juice
    Vanilla ice cream

In a microwave-safe bowl, combine unsweetened chocolate and butter. Cover and cook on high for 1 minute; stir. Microwave 1 minute longer; stir until smooth. Cool for 10 minutes.

In a mixing bowl, beat eggs, 1-3/4 cups sugar and vanilla for 3 minutes. Beat in melted chocolate. Add flour; beat until combined. Stir in chocolate chips. Pour into two greased 9-in. pie plates. Bake at 350° for 25-30 minutes or until a toothpick inserted in the center comes out clean. Cool on wire racks.

In a bowl, combine raspberries and remaining sugar; mash gently. Place mixture in a sieve and press with the back of a spoon; discard seeds and pulp. Add lemon juice to raspberry puree; refrigerate until serving.

Cut brownies into wedges; serve with ice cream and raspberry sauce. **Yield:** 12-16 servings.

## Merry Cherry Bars

Joan Wood, Shelton, Washington

Flaked coconut and chopped nuts are tasty companions for the maraschino cherries in these festive baked goods. Add them to your holiday cookie tray.

        1    cup all-purpose flour
        3    tablespoons confectioners' sugar
      1/2    cup butter, cubed
        1    cup sugar
      1/4    cup all-purpose flour
      1/2    teaspoon baking powder
      1/4    teaspoon salt
        2    eggs, lightly beaten
        1    teaspoon vanilla extract
      3/4    cup chopped nuts
      1/2    cup flaked coconut
      1/2    cup maraschino cherries, quartered

In a large bowl, combine flour and confectioners' sugar; cut in butter until the mixture resembles coarse crumbs. Pat into a greased 11-in. x 7-in. x 2-in. baking pan. Bake at 375° for 10 minutes or until edges are lightly browned. Cool.

In a large bowl, combine the sugar, flour, baking powder and salt. Add eggs and vanilla. Fold in nuts, coconut and cherries; spread over crust.

Bake at 375° for 17-22 minutes or until lightly browned. Cool before cutting. **Yield:** 1-1/2 dozen.

## Cherry Streusel Squares

T. Moore, Oaklyn, New Jersey

I don't think food should take longer to make than it does to eat, so I love these time-saving bar cookies. At Christmas, I like to use red and green cherries.

        1    cup butter, softened
      1/3    cup packed brown sugar
        1    teaspoon vanilla extract
      1/4    teaspoon almond extract
        2    cups all-purpose flour
        1    cup chopped pecans
        1    cup finely chopped candied *or*
             maraschino cherries
    STREUSEL:
        1    cup all-purpose flour
      1/2    cup sugar
        6    tablespoons cold butter, cubed
      1/2    cup chopped pecans

In a large mixing bowl, cream butter and brown sugar until light and fluffy. Beat in extracts. Gradually add flour. Stir in pecans and cherries. Spread into an ungreased 13-in. x 9-in. x 2-in. baking pan.

In a small bowl, combine the flour and sugar; cut in butter until mixture resembles coarse crumbs. Add pecans. Sprinkle over dough.

Bake at 350° for 30-35 minutes or until very light brown. Cool on a wire rack. Cut into 1-1/2-in. squares. **Yield:** 4 dozen.

crimson crumble bars

## Fruity Brownie Pizza

Nancy Johnson, Laverne, Oklahoma

A basic brownie mix helps to quickly create this luscious dessert that's sure to impress company. Sometimes, I add mandarin oranges for even more color.

  1   package fudge brownie mix (8-inch square pan size)
  1   package (8 ounces) cream cheese, softened
1/3  cup sugar
  1   can (8 ounces) pineapple tidbits
  1   small firm banana, sliced
  1   medium kiwifruit, peeled and sliced
  1   cup sliced fresh strawberries
1/4  cup chopped pecans
  1   square (1 ounce) semisweet chocolate
  1   tablespoon butter

Prepare brownie mix according to package directions. Spread the batter into a greased 12-in. pizza pan. Bake at 375° for 15-20 minutes or until a toothpick inserted near the center comes out clean. Cool completely.

Meanwhile, in a large mixing bowl, beat cream cheese and sugar until smooth. Spread over crust. Drain pineapple, reserving juice. Toss the banana slices with the juice; drain well.

Arrange the banana, kiwi, strawberries and pineapple over cream cheese layer; sprinkle with pecans. In a microwave, melt chocolate and butter; stir until smooth. Drizzle over fruit. Cover and refrigerate for 1 hour. **Yield:** 12-14 servings.

## Crimson Crumble Bars

Paula Eriksen, Palm Harbor, Florida

Baking is my favorite pastime. These moist cranberry bites have a refreshing sweet-tart taste and a pleasant crumble topping. They're great as a coffee snack or an anytime treat.

  1   cup sugar
  2   teaspoons cornstarch
  2   cups fresh *or* frozen cranberries
  1   can (8 ounces) unsweetened crushed pineapple, undrained
  1   cup all-purpose flour
2/3  cup old-fashioned oats
2/3  cup packed brown sugar
1/4  teaspoon salt
1/2  cup cold butter, cubed
1/2  cup chopped pecans

In a large saucepan, combine the sugar, cornstarch, cranberries and pineapple; bring to a boil, stirring often. Reduce heat; cover and simmer for 10-15 minutes or until the berries pop. Remove from the heat.

In a large bowl, combine the flour, oats, brown sugar and salt. Cut in butter until mixture resembles coarse crumbs. Stir in the pecans. Set aside 1-1/2 cups for topping.

Press remaining crumb mixture onto the bottom of a 13-in. x 9-in. x 2-in. baking pan coated with nonstick cooking spray. Bake at 350° for 8-10 minutes or until firm; cook for 10 minutes.

Pour fruit filling over crust. Sprinkle with reserved crumb mixture. Bake for 25-30 minutes longer or until golden brown. Cool on a wire rack. **Yield:** 2 dozen.

fruity brownie pizza

## Fruit 'n Nut Spice Bars
*Loretta Dunn, Lyons, Oregon*

Chock-full of flavor from cherries, honey, spices, walnuts and chocolate chips, my special snacks are topped off with a drizzle of vanilla glaze.

|       |                                         |
|-------|-----------------------------------------|
| 3/4   | cup chopped maraschino cherries         |
| 2-1/4 | cups all-purpose flour, *divided*       |
| 1     | package (8 ounces) cream cheese, softened |
| 1/2   | cup butter, softened                    |
| 1-1/2 | cups packed brown sugar                 |
| 1     | egg                                     |
| 1/4   | cup honey                               |
| 1-1/2 | teaspoons baking powder                 |
| 1     | teaspoon salt                           |
| 1     | teaspoon ground cinnamon                |
| 1     | teaspoon ground nutmeg                  |
| 1     | cup chopped walnuts                     |
| 3/4   | cup miniature chocolate chips           |
| 1-1/3 | cups confectioners' sugar               |
| 2     | tablespoons milk                        |
| 1/4   | teaspoon vanilla extract                |

In a small bowl, toss cherries with 1/4 cup flour; set aside. In a large mixing bowl, beat cream cheese, butter and brown sugar until smooth. Beat in egg and honey. Combine the baking powder, salt, cinnamon, nutmeg and remaining flour; add to creamed mixture. Stir in nuts, chocolate chips and reserved cherries.

Spread into a greased 15-in. x 10-in. x 1-in. baking pan. Bake at 350° for 30-35 minutes or until golden brown. In a small bowl, combine the confectioners' sugar, milk and vanilla until smooth; drizzle over warm bars. Cool on a wire rack for 1 hour. **Yield:** 4 dozen.

fruit 'n nut spice bars

strawberry oatmeal bars

## Strawberry Oatmeal Bars
*Flo Burtnett, Gage, Oklahoma*

A fruity filling and fluffy coconut topping make these bars truly one of a kind. They really dress up my cookie trays.

|       |                           |
|-------|---------------------------|
| 1-1/4 | cups all-purpose flour    |
| 1-1/4 | cups quick-cooking oats   |
| 1/2   | cup sugar                 |
| 1/2   | teaspoon baking powder    |
| 1/4   | teaspoon salt             |
| 3/4   | cup butter, melted        |
| 2     | teaspoons vanilla extract |
| 1     | cup strawberry preserves  |
| 1/2   | cup flaked coconut        |

In a bowl, combine dry ingredients. Add butter and vanilla; stir until crumbly. Set aside 1 cup. Press remaining crumb mixture evenly into an ungreased 13-in. x 9-in. x 2-in. baking pan. Spread preserves over crust. Combine coconut and reserved crumb mixture; sprinkle over preserves.

Bake at 350° for 25-30 minutes or until coconut is lightly browned. Cool. **Yield:** 3 dozen.

## Banana Cocoa Brownies
*Rebecca Luginbill, Pandora, Ohio*

Banana pairs great with chocolate, making these brownies an all-time favorite in my home. I hope you enjoy them, as much as we do.

|       |                                       |
|-------|---------------------------------------|
| 1     | cup quick-cooking oats                |
| 1     | cup boiling water                     |
| 4     | egg whites                            |
| 1-1/2 | cups mashed ripe bananas (about 3 medium) |
| 3/4   | cup packed brown sugar                |
| 1/2   | cup sugar                             |

2 tablespoons vegetable oil
1 teaspoon vanilla extract
1 cup all-purpose flour
1/4 cup baking cocoa
1 teaspoon baking soda
1/2 teaspoon salt

In a small bowl, combine oats and boiling water; let stand for 5 minutes. In a large mixing bowl, beat the egg whites, bananas, sugars, oil and vanilla until blended. Combine the dry ingredients; gradually add to creamed mixture. Stir in the oat mixture.

Spread into a 13-in. x 9-in. x 2-in. pan coated with non-stick cooking spray. Bake at 350° for 20-25 minutes or until a toothpick inserted near the center comes out clean (do not overbake). Cool on a wire rack. Cut into bars. **Yield:** 4 dozen.

## Lime Cooler Bars

Dorothy Anderson, Ottawa, Kansas

My family says this is one of their favorites. I guarantee it will get thumbs-up approval from your gang, too. Lime juice puts a tangy twist on these tantalizing bars, offering a burst of citrus flavor in every mouth-watering bite.

2-1/2 cups all-purpose flour, *divided*
1/2 cup confectioners' sugar
3/4 cup cold butter, cubed
4 eggs
2 cups sugar
1/3 cup lime juice
1/2 teaspoon grated lime peel
1/2 teaspoon baking powder
Additional confectioners' sugar

In a large bowl, combine 2 cups flour and confectioners' sugar; cut in butter until mixture resembles coarse crumbs. Pat into a greased 13-in. x 9-in. x 2-in. baking pan.

Bake at 350° for 20 minutes or until lightly browned.

In a large bowl, whisk the eggs, sugar, lime juice and peel until frothy. Combine the baking powder and remaining flour; whisk in egg mixture. Pour over hot crust.

Bake for 20-25 minutes or until light golden brown. Cool on a wire rack. Dust with confectioners' sugar. Cut into squares. **Yield:** 3 dozen.

## Spiced Apple Bars

Evelyn Winchester, Hilton, New York

I bake chopped walnuts and hearty oats into these apple-cinnamon squares. They are delightful in autumn and make a nice change from apple pie.

1/2 cup butter, softened
1 cup sugar
2 eggs
1 cup all-purpose flour
1 cup quick-cooking oats
1 tablespoon baking cocoa
1 teaspoon baking powder
1 teaspoon ground cinnamon
1/2 teaspoon baking soda
1/2 teaspoon salt
1/2 teaspoon ground nutmeg
1/4 teaspoon ground cloves
1-1/2 cups diced peeled tart apple
1/2 cup chopped walnuts
Confectioners' sugar

In a large mixing bowl, cream butter and sugar until light and fluffy. Add the eggs, one at a time, beating well after each. Combine dry ingredients; gradually add to creamed mixture. Stir in apple and nuts.

Spread into a greased 13-in. x 9-in. x 2-in. baking pan. Bake at 375° for 20-25 minutes or until a toothpick comes out clean. Cool. Dust with confectioners' sugar. Cut into bars. **Yield:** about 2-1/2 dozen.

lime cooler bars

### Brownie Point

"Growing tired of the ordinary taste that my packaged brownie mix provided, I decided to use half of the water called for on the box and make up the difference with raspberry syrup," explains Sacramento, California's Sheila Bliss. "Not only did the syrup add a fun hint of raspberry, but it made the brownies very moist."

# Chapter 4

p. 64

p. 54

p. 55

p. 61

p. 66

# Caramel, Nuts & More

Ooey-gooey and completely irresistible, these mouth-watering delights feature items such as caramels, pecans, chocolate chips and other delicious surprises.

## Peanut Butter Caramel Bars

Lee Ann Karnowski, Stevens Point, Wisconsin

When my husband and our three sons sit down to dinner, they ask, "What's for dessert?" I have a happy group of guys when I report that these rich bars are on the menu. They're chock-full of yummy ingredients.

      1  package (18-1/4 ounces) yellow cake mix
    1/2  cup butter, softened
      1  egg
     20  miniature peanut butter cups, chopped
      2  tablespoons cornstarch
      1  jar (12-1/4 ounces) caramel ice cream topping
    1/4  cup peanut butter
    1/2  cup salted peanuts
**TOPPING:**
      1  can (16 ounces) milk chocolate frosting
    1/2  cup chopped salted peanuts

In a large mixing bowl, combine the cake mix, butter and egg; beat until no longer crumbly, about 3 minutes. Stir in the peanut butter cups.

Press into a greased 13-in. x 9-in. x 2-in. baking pan. Bake at 350° for 18-22 minutes or until lightly browned.

Meanwhile, in a large saucepan, combine the cornstarch, caramel topping and peanut butter; stir until smooth. Cook over low heat for about 25- 27 minutes or until mixture comes to a boil; stirring occasionally. Remove from the heat; stir in peanuts.

Spread evenly over warm crust. Bake 6-7 minutes longer or until almost set. Cool completely on a wire rack. Spread with frosting; sprinkle with peanuts. Cover and refrigerate for at least 1 hour before cutting. Store in the refrigerator. **Yield:** about 3 dozen.

peanut butter caramel bars

caramel corn chocolate bars

## Caramel Corn Chocolate Bars

Jean Roczniak, Rochester, Minnesota

Caramel corn makes these change-of-pace bars a breeze to whip up. Chocolate chips add the perfect touch.

      5  cups caramel corn
      1  cup chopped pecans
      1  package (10-1/2 ounces) miniature marshmallows, *divided*
    1/4  cup butter, cubed
    1/2  cup semisweet chocolate chips

In a large bowl, combine caramel corn, pecans and 1 cup marshmallows. In a small heavy saucepan, melt butter over low heat. Add chips and remaining marshmallows; cook and stir until smooth.

Pour over caramel corn mixture; toss to coat. With buttered hands, press into a greased 13-in. x 9-in. x 2-in. pan. Cool. Cut with a serrated knife. **Yield:** 2 dozen.

## Gooey Chip Bars

Beatriz Boggs, Delray Beach, Florida

You'll never believe how easy these four-ingredient bars are to assemble, you'll turn to them time and again.

      2  cups graham cracker crumbs
      1  can (14 ounces) sweetened condensed milk
      1  cup (6 ounces) semisweet chocolate chips, *divided*
    1/2  cup chopped walnuts *or* pecans, optional

In a large bowl, combine cracker crumbs and milk. Stir in 1/2 cup chocolate chips and nuts if desired (batter will be very thick).

Pat into the bottom of a well-greased 8-in. square baking pan. Sprinkle with remaining chocolate chips. Bake at 350° for 20-25 minutes or until golden brown. Cool on a wire rack; cut into bars. **Yield:** 1-1/2 dozen.

## Peanut Mallow Bars

Claudia Ruiss, Massapequa, New York

Searching for the perfect combination of salty and sweet sensations? Well, look no further! Salted peanuts and rich caramel topping join marshmallow creme and brown sugar in these irresistible chewy bars. You won't be able to stop at just one!

      1   cup chopped salted peanuts
    3/4   cup all-purpose flour
    3/4   cup quick-cooking oats
    2/3   cup packed brown sugar
    1/2   teaspoon salt
    1/2   teaspoon baking soda
      1   egg, lightly beaten
    1/3   cup cold butter
TOPPING:
      1   jar (7 ounces) marshmallow creme
    2/3   cup caramel ice cream topping
  1-3/4   cups salted peanuts

In a large bowl, combine the peanuts, flour, oats, sugar, salt and baking soda; stir in the egg. Cut in butter until crumbly. Press into a greased 13-in. x 9-in. x 2-in. baking pan. Bake at 350° for 8-10 minutes or until lightly browned.

Spoon marshmallow creme over hot crust; carefully spread evenly. Drizzle with the caramel topping; sprinkle with peanuts. Bake for 15-20 minutes or until lightly browned. Cool on a wire rack. Cut into bars. **Yield:** 3 dozen.

***Editor's Note:*** *This recipe was tested with an 850-watt microwave.*

peanut mallow bars

walnut cookie strips

## Walnut Cookie Strips

June Grimm, San Rafael, California

This recipe is a classic in our home. It will be enjoyed by both kids and adults.

    1/2   cup all-purpose flour
    1/8   teaspoon salt
    1/4   cup cold butter, cubed
FILLING:
      1   egg
    3/4   cup packed brown sugar
      2   tablespoons all-purpose flour
    1/2   teaspoon vanilla extract
    1/8   teaspoon baking powder
    1/2   cup chopped walnuts
    1/4   cup flaked coconut
FROSTING:
    3/4   cup confectioners' sugar
      1   tablespoon butter, softened
      1   tablespoon orange juice
    1/2   teaspoon lemon juice
    1/4   cup chopped walnuts

In a small bowl, combine flour and salt; cut in butter until crumbly. Press into a greased 9-in. x 5-in. x 3-in. loaf pan. Bake at 350° for 15 minutes or until lightly browned.

Meanwhile, in a small mixing bowl, beat egg. Beat in the brown sugar, flour, vanilla and baking powder. Stir in nuts and coconut. Pour over hot crust. Bake 15 minutes longer or until set. Cool completely on a wire rack.

For frosting, in a small mixing bowl, beat the confectioners' sugar, butter and juices until smooth. Spread over filling; sprinkle with nuts. Cover and refrigerate for 1-2 hours or until frosting is set. Store in the refrigerator. **Yield:** 2 dozen.

caramel brownie pizza

## Caramel Brownie Pizza

Amy Branson, Bristol, Virginia

This moist fudgy pizza, topped with caramel, chips and nuts, is sure to satisfy. To prevent the tips of wedges from breaking when serving, I keep the topping slightly thinner in the center.

> 1 package brownie mix
>   (13-inch x 9-inch size)
> 1/2 cup caramel apple dip
> 1/2 cup miniature chocolate chips
> 1/4 cup chopped pecans

Prepare brownie mix according to package directions. Coat a 12-in. pizza pan with nonstick cooking spray. Spread batter over pan to within 1 in. of the edge.

Bake at 350° for 25-30 minutes or until a toothpick inserted 2 in. from edge comes out clean. Cool completely on a wire rack. Spread caramel apple dip over the top; sprinkle with chocolate chips and pecans. **Yield:** 12 servings.

## Toffee Nut Squares

Anna Marie Cobb, Pearland, Texas

Here's a yummy recipe that my mother passed along. Packed with coconut and nuts, the soft but chewy bars will be a hit at your next party.

> 1/2 cup butter, softened
> 1/2 cup packed brown sugar
>   1 cup all-purpose flour
> 1/4 cup whipping cream
> FILLING:
>   1 cup packed brown sugar
>   2 eggs
>   1 teaspoon vanilla extract
>   2 tablespoons all-purpose flour
>   1 teaspoon baking powder

> 1/4 teaspoon salt
>   1 cup flaked coconut
>   1 cup chopped nuts

In a large mixing bowl, cream the butter and brown sugar until light and fluffy. Gradually add flour. Add cream, 1 tablespoon at a time, until a soft dough forms. Press into an ungreased 9-in. square baking pan. Bake at 350° for 15 minutes.

Meanwhile, in a small mixing bowl, beat the brown sugar, eggs and vanilla until blended. Combine the flour, baking powder and salt; gradually add to mixture. Stir in coconut and nuts.

Spread over the crust. Bake for 25-20 minutes or until a toothpick inserted near the center comes out clean. Cool on a wire rack before cutting. **Yield:** about 1-1/2 dozen.

## Macadamia Chip Brownies

Lucile Cline, Wichita, Kansas

With two kinds of chocolate and macadamia nuts, there's no need to frost these scrumptious bars! I like to make them for special occasions.

> 1/3 cup butter
>   4 squares (1 ounce *each*) white baking chocolate
>   2 eggs
>   1 cup sugar
>   1 teaspoon vanilla extract
>   1 cup all-purpose flour
> 1/4 teaspoon salt
> 1/2 cup chopped macadamia nuts
> 1/2 cup milk chocolate chips

In a saucepan over low heat, melt butter and white chocolate; remove from the heat. In a bowl, combine the eggs, sugar and vanilla. Add the chocolate mixture, flour and salt; mix well. Stir in nuts and chocolate chips.

Pour into a greased 9-in. square baking pan. Bake at 325° for 30-35 minutes or until top is lightly browned. Cool on a wire rack. Cut into bars. **Yield:** 1-1/2 dozen.

macadamia chip brownies

pecan pie bars

## Pecan Pie Bars

Clara Honeyager, North Prairie, Wisconsin

I love to cook large quantities and do most of the cooking for our church functions. People seem to enjoy these scrumptious bars even more than old-fashioned pecan pie.

|     |                          |
| --- | ------------------------ |
| 6   | cups all-purpose flour   |
| 1-1/2 | cups sugar             |
| 1   | teaspoon salt            |
| 2   | cups cold butter, cubed  |

FILLING:

|     |                        |
| --- | ---------------------- |
| 8   | eggs                   |
| 3   | cups sugar             |
| 3   | cups corn syrup        |
| 1/2 | cup butter, melted     |
| 3   | teaspoons vanilla extract |
| 5   | cups chopped pecans    |

In a large bowl, combine the flour, sugar and salt. Cut in butter until crumbly. Press onto the bottom and up the sides of two greased 15-in. x 10-in. x 1-in. baking pans. Bake at 350° for 18-22 minutes or until crust edges are beginning to brown and bottom is set.

For filling, combine the eggs, sugar, corn syrup, butter and vanilla in a large bowl. Stir in pecans. Pour over crust.

Bake 25-30 minutes longer or until edges are firm and center is almost set. Cool on wire racks. Cut into bars. Refrigerate until serving. **Yield:** 6-8 dozen.

## No-Bake Peanut Brownies

Connie Ward, Mt. Pleasant, Iowa

Chopped peanuts add a delightful flavor to these no-fuss brownies. I like the fact that you can prepare the treats without heating up the oven.

|     |                          |
| --- | ------------------------ |
| 4   | cups graham cracker crumbs |
| 1   | cup chopped peanuts      |
| 1/2 | cup confectioners' sugar |

|     |                                        |
| --- | -------------------------------------- |
| 1/4 | cup peanut butter                      |
| 2   | cups (12 ounces) semisweet chocolate chips |
| 1   | cup evaporated milk                    |
| 1   | teaspoon vanilla extract               |

In a large bowl, combine the crumbs, peanuts, sugar and peanut butter until crumbly. In a small saucepan, melt the chocolate chips and milk over low heat, stirring constantly until smooth. Remove from the heat; add vanilla. Set aside 1/2 cup.

Pour remaining chocolate mixture over crumb mixture and stir until well blended. Spread evenly in a greased 9-in. square baking pan. Frost with the reserved chocolate mixture. Cover and refrigerate for 1 hour. **Yield**: 2-1/2 dozen.

## Caramel Cashew Brownies

Judy High, Berryville, Arkansas

I always have my eye out for a good recipe, like the one for these marvelous golden brownies. It's hard to eat just one!

|     |                              |
| --- | ---------------------------- |
| 18  | caramels                     |
| 1/3 | cup butter                   |
| 2   | tablespoons milk             |
| 3/4 | cup sugar                    |
| 2   | eggs                         |
| 1/2 | teaspoon vanilla extract     |
| 1   | cup all-purpose flour        |
| 1/2 | teaspoon baking powder       |
| 1/4 | teaspoon salt                |
| 1   | cup chopped salted cashews   |

In a saucepan, cook and stir the caramels, butter and milk over low heat until the caramels are melted and mixture is smooth. Remove from the heat; stir in sugar.

Combine eggs and vanilla; stir into caramel mixture. Combine the flour, baking powder and salt; stir into caramel mixture until blended. Fold in cashews.

Transfer to a greased 9-in. square baking pan. Bake at 350° for 24-28 minutes or until a toothpick inserted near the center comes out clean. Cool on a wire rack. Cut into bars. **Yield:** 25 brownies.

caramel cashew brownies

## Peppermint Patty Brownies

Clara Bakke, Coon Rapids, Minnesota

I add a special ingredient to these sweet and fudgy brownies. A layer of mint patties provides the refreshing surprise tucked inside.

- 1-1/2  cups butter, softened
- 3  cups sugar
- 5  eggs
- 1  tablespoon vanilla extract
- 2  cups all-purpose flour
- 1  cup baking cocoa
- 1  teaspoon baking powder
- 1  teaspoon salt
- 1  package (13 ounces) chocolate-covered peppermint patties

In a large mixing bowl, cream butter and sugar until light and fluffy. Add eggs, one at a time, beating well after each addition. Beat in vanilla. Combine the dry ingredients; add to creamed mixture and mix well.

Spread about two-thirds of the batter in a greased 13-in. x 9-in. x 2-in. baking pan. Arrange peppermint patties over top. Carefully spread remaining batter over patties. Bake at 350° for 35-40 minutes or until edges begin to pull away from sides of pan and a toothpick inserted near the center comes out clean (top will appear uneven). Cool completely on a wire rack. Cut into bars. **Yield:** 2 to 2-1/2 dozen.

## Rocky Road Brownies

Rita Lenes, Kent, Washington

Anyone who likes rocky road ice cream should sample these moist, chocolate brownies loaded with goodies. They're great for children's parties.

peppermint patty brownies

- 3/4  cup butter, cubed
- 4  squares (1 ounce *each*) unsweetened chocolate
- 4  eggs
- 2  cups sugar
- 1  teaspoon vanilla extract
- 1  cup all-purpose flour
- 2  cups miniature marshmallows
- 1  cup (6 ounces) semisweet chocolate chips
- 1  cup chopped walnuts

In a large saucepan over low heat, melt butter and chocolate, stir until smooth; cool for 10 minutes.

In a large mixing bowl, beat the eggs, sugar and vanilla. Stir in chocolate mixture. Gradually add the flour until well combined.

Spread into a greased 13-in. x 9-in. x 2-in. baking pan. Bake at 350° for 25-30 minutes or until a toothpick inserted near the center comes out clean. Sprinkle with marshmallows, chocolate chips and walnuts; bake 4 minutes longer. Cool on a wire rack. **Yield:** 2 dozen.

## Orange Slice Bars

Elaine Norton, Sandusky, Michigan

Walnuts and strips of orange candy slices make a unique pairing in my change-of-pace bars. They travel well, making them a great contribution to potlucks and get-togethers.

- 1  pound orange candy slices, cut into 1/8-inch strips
- 6  tablespoons hot water
- 1/2  cup butter, softened
- 2-1/4  cups packed brown sugar
- 4  eggs
- 1  teaspoon vanilla extract
- 2-1/2  cups all-purpose flour
- 2  teaspoons baking powder

rocky road brownies

1/2 teaspoon salt
1/2 cup chopped walnuts
Confectioners' sugar

In a large bowl, combine candy and water. Cover and refrigerate overnight; drain well and set aside.

In a large mixing bowl, cream butter and brown sugar until light and fluffy. Add eggs, one at a time, beating well after each. Beat in vanilla. Combine the flour, baking powder and salt; gradually add to creamed mixture. Fold in walnuts and candy.

Spread into a greased 15-in. x 10-in. x 1-in. baking pan. Bake at 350° for 25-30 minutes or until golden brown. Cool on a wire rack. Dust with confectioners' sugar. Cut into bars. **Yield**: about 4 dozen.

## Triple-Nut Diamonds

Darlene King, Estevan, Saskatchewan

My dad has always been crazy about nuts, so when I came upon this recipe, I knew I had to try it. The diamond shape is a nice addition to our Christmas cookie tray.

1 cup all-purpose flour
1/2 cup sugar
1/2 cup cold butter, *divided*
1/2 cup packed brown sugar
2 tablespoons honey
1/4 cup heavy whipping cream
2/3 cup *each* chopped pecans, walnuts and
 almonds

Line a greased 9-in. square baking pan with foil; grease the foil and set aside. In a bowl, combine the flour and sugar. Cut in 1/4 cup butter until mixture resembles coarse crumbs; press into prepared pan. Bake at 350° for 10 minutes.

triple-nut diamonds

pecan-toffee bars

In a saucepan, heat the brown sugar, honey and remaining butter until bubbly. Boil for 1 minute. Remove from the heat; stir in cream and nuts. Pour over crust. Bake at 350° for 16-20 minutes or until surface is bubbly. Cool on a wire rack.

Refrigerate for 30 minutes. Using foil, lift bars out of the pan; cut into diamonds. **Yield:** 4 dozen.

## Pecan-Toffee Bars

Carolyn Custer, Clifton Park, New York

These bars are rich and delicious—just like pecan pie with a little surprise of toffee. They're perfect for taking to casual gatherings.

2 cups all-purpose flour
1/2 cup confectioners' sugar
1 cup butter, softened
1 can (14 ounces) sweetened condensed milk
1 egg
1 teaspoon vanilla extract
Pinch salt
1 package (10 ounces) English toffee bits *or*
 1 package (7-1/2 ounces) almond brickle chips
1 cup chopped pecans

In a large bowl, combine flour and sugar. Cut in butter until mixture resembles coarse meal. Press firmly onto the bottom of a greased 13-in. x 9-in. x 2-in. baking dish. Bake at 350° for 15 minutes.

Meanwhile, in large mixing bowl, beat the milk, egg, vanilla and salt until smooth. Stir in toffee chips and pecans; spread evenly over baked crust.

Bake for 20-25 minutes longer or until lightly browned. Cool. Cover and chill; cut into bars. Store in refrigerator. **Yield:** 4 dozen.

rustic nut bars

stir for 1 minute or until smooth. Remove from the heat; stir in the hazelnuts, almonds, cashews and pistachios. Spread over crust.

Bake at 375° for 15-20 minutes or until topping is bubbly. Cool completely on a wire rack. Using foil, lift bars out of pan. Discard foil; cut into squares. **Yield:** about 3 dozen.

## Coconut Granola Bars

Maria Cade, Fort Rock, Oregon

These quick-to-fix bars are wholesome and delicious. I sometimes make them for bake sales.

- 3/4 cup packed brown sugar
- 2/3 cup peanut butter
- 1/2 cup corn syrup
- 1/2 cup butter, melted
- 2 teaspoons vanilla extract
- 3 cups old-fashioned oats
- 1 cup (6 ounces) semisweet chocolate chips
- 1/2 cup flaked coconut
- 1/2 cup sunflower kernels
- 1/3 cup toasted wheat germ
- 2 teaspoons sesame seeds

In a large bowl, combine brown sugar, peanut butter, corn syrup, butter and vanilla. Combine the remaining ingredients; add to peanut butter mixture and stir to coat. Press into two greased 13-in. x 9-in. x 2-in. baking pans. Bake at 350° for 25-30 minutes or until golden brown. Cool on wire racks. Cut into bars. **Yield:** 3 dozen.

## Rustic Nut Bars

Barbara Driscoll, West Allis, Wisconsin

Everyone will crunch with joy when they bite into these bars. The shortbread-like crust and the wildly nutty topping are real people pleasers.

- 1 tablespoon plus 3/4 cup cold butter, *divided*
- 2-1/3 cups all-purpose flour
- 1/2 cup sugar
- 1/2 teaspoon baking powder
- 1/2 teaspoon salt
- 1 egg, lightly beaten

TOPPING:
- 2/3 cup honey
- 1/2 cup packed brown sugar
- 1/4 teaspoon salt
- 6 tablespoons butter, cubed
- 2 tablespoons heavy whipping cream
- 1 cup chopped hazelnuts, toasted
- 1 cup roasted salted almonds
- 1 cup salted cashews, toasted
- 1 cup pistachios, toasted

Line a 13-in. x 9-in. x 2-in. baking pan with foil; grease the foil with 1 tablespoon butter. Set aside.

In a large bowl, combine the flour, sugar, baking powder and salt; cut in remaining butter until mixture resembles coarse crumbs. Stir in egg until blended (mixture will be dry).

Press firmly onto the bottom of prepared pan. Bake at 375° for 18-20 minutes or until edges are golden brown. Cool on a wire rack.

In a large heavy saucepan, bring the honey, brown sugar and salt to a boil over medium heat until sugar is smooth; stirring often. Boil without stirring for 2 minutes. Add butter and cream. Bring to a boil; cook and

## Chippy Blond Brownies

Anna Jean Allen, West Liberty, Kentucky

If you love chocolate and butterscotch, you won't be able to resist these chewy goodies. Everyone, young and old, enjoys these sweet treats.

chippy blond brownies

6 tablespoons butter, softened
1 cup packed brown sugar
2 eggs
1 teaspoon vanilla extract
1-1/4 cups all-purpose flour
1 teaspoon baking powder
1/2 teaspoon salt
1 cup (6 ounces) semisweet chocolate chips
1/2 cup chopped pecans

In a large mixing bowl, cream butter and brown sugar. Add the eggs, one at a time, beating well after each addition. Beat in vanilla. Combine the flour, baking powder and salt; gradually add to creamed mixture. Stir in the chocolate chips and pecans.

Spread into a greased 11-in. x 7-in. x 2-in. baking pan. Bake at 350° for 25-30 minutes or until a toothpick inserted near the center comes out clean. Cool on a wire rack. **Yield:** 2 dozen.

## Caramel Macadamia Nut Brownies

Jamie Bursell, Juneau, Alaska

One bite and you'll agree this is the most delectable brownie you've ever tasted! Eat it with a fork to savor every last morsel of chocolate, caramel and nuts.

1 teaspoon plus 3/4 cup butter, *divided*
3 squares (1 ounce *each*) unsweetened chocolate
3 eggs
1-1/2 cups packed brown sugar
2 teaspoons vanilla extract
3/4 cup all-purpose flour
1/4 teaspoon baking soda
CARAMEL LAYER:
3/4 cup sugar
3 tablespoons water
1/4 cup heavy whipping cream
2 tablespoons butter
TOPPING:
1-1/2 cups semisweet chocolate chips
1 cup milk chocolate chips
1 jar (3-1/2 ounces) macadamia nuts, coarsely chopped

Line a 9-in. square baking pan with foil; grease the foil with 1 teaspoon butter and set aside. In a microwave-safe bowl, melt chocolate and remaining butter; stir until smooth. Cool for 10 minutes. In a large mixing bowl, beat eggs and brown sugar until blended; beat in chocolate mixture and vanilla. Combine flour and baking soda; gradually add to chocolate mixture.

Pour into prepared pan. Bake at 325° for 40 minutes or until a toothpick inserted near the center comes out with moist crumbs (do not overbake). Cool on a wire rack.

In a large heavy saucepan, combine sugar and water. Cook and stir over medium heat for 4-5 minutes or until sugar is dissolved. Cook over medium-high heat without stirring until syrup is golden, about 5 minutes; remove from the heat.

black walnut brownies

In a small saucepan, heat cream over low heat until small bubbles form around edge of pan. Gradually stir cream into syrup (mixture will boil up). Cook and stir over low heat until blended. Stir in butter until melted. Remove from the heat; cool slightly.

Pour over brownies to within 1/4 in. of edges. Sprinkle with chips and nuts. Bake at 325° for 5 minutes (do not let chips melt completely). Cool completely on a wire rack. Refrigerate for 4 hours. Lift out of the pan; remove foil. Cut into bars. **Yield:** 20 brownies.

## Black Walnut Brownies

Catherine Berra Bleem, Walsh, Illinois

A handful of ingredients help me bake up these treats in no time. The black walnuts are a great change of pace, but feel free to use whatever variety your family enjoys most.

1 cup sugar
1/4 cup vegetable oil
2 eggs
1 teaspoon vanilla extract
1/2 cup all-purpose flour
2 tablespoons baking cocoa
1/2 teaspoon salt
1/2 cup chopped black walnuts

In a small mixing bowl, beat sugar and oil until blended. Beat in eggs and vanilla. Combine the flour, cocoa and salt; gradually add to sugar mixture until well blended. Stir in walnuts.

Pour into a greased 8-in. square baking pan. Bake at 350° for 30-35 minutes or until a toothpick comes out clean. Cool on a wire rack. **Yield:** 16 servings.

## Peanut Butter Brownies

Margaret McNeil, Memphis, Tennessee

The combination of peanut butter and chocolate makes these brownies a real crowd-pleaser. They're so good, they won a ribbon at a local fair.

  3   eggs
  1   cup butter, melted
  2   teaspoons vanilla extract
  2   cups sugar
1-1/4   cups all-purpose flour
 3/4   cup baking cocoa
 1/2   teaspoon baking powder
 1/4   teaspoon salt
  1   cup milk chocolate chips
FILLING:
  2   packages (8 ounces *each*) cream cheese, softened
 1/2   cup creamy peanut butter
 1/4   cup sugar
  1   egg
  2   tablespoons milk

In a large mixing bowl, beat the eggs, butter and vanilla until smooth. Combine the dry ingredients; gradually add to egg mixture. Stir in chocolate chips. Set aside 1 cup for topping. Spread remaining batter into a greased 13-in. x 9-in. x 2-in. baking pan.

In a small mixing bowl, beat the cream cheese, peanut butter and sugar until smooth. Beat in egg and milk on low just until combined. Carefully spread over batter. Drop reserved batter by tablespoonfuls over filling. Cut through batter with a knife to swirl.

Bake at 350° for 35-40 minutes or until a toothpick inserted in the center comes out clean. Cool on a wire rack. Chill until serving. **Yield:** 3 dozen.

***Editor's Note:*** *Reduced-fat or generic brands of peanut butter are not recommended for this recipe.*

peanut butter brownies

golden m&m bars

## Golden M&M Bars

Martha Haseman, Hinckley, Illinois

Our family loves to take drives, and I often bring these bars along for snacking in the car.

 1/2   cup butter, softened
 3/4   cup sugar
 3/4   cup packed brown sugar
  2   eggs
  2   teaspoons vanilla extract
1-1/2   cups all-purpose flour
  1   teaspoon baking powder
 1/2   teaspoon salt
  1   cup vanilla *or* white chips
1-3/4   cups plain M&Ms, *divided*

In a large mixing bowl, cream butter and sugars until light and fluffy. Beat in eggs and vanilla. Combine the flour, baking powder and salt; gradually add to the creamed mixture. Stir in chips and 1 cup of M&Ms.

Spoon into a greased 13-in. x 9-in. x 2-in. baking pan; spread evenly in pan. Sprinkle with the remaining M&Ms. Bake at 350° for 25-30 minutes or until golden brown. Cool on a wire rack. Cut into bars. **Yield:** 2 dozen.

## Heavenly Hash Bars

Peg Wilson, Elm Creek, Nebraska

Chock-full of chips, nuts and mini marshmallows, these rich bars are a cinch to stir up. They make great Christmas treats, but I prepare them year-round.

  1   package (16 ounces) miniature marshmallows
  1   can (11-1/2 ounces) mixed nuts
  2   cups (12 ounces) semisweet chocolate chips
  2   cups butterscotch chips
  1   cup peanut butter

Sprinkle marshmallows and nuts in a greased 13-in. x 9-in. x 2-in. pan; set aside. In a small saucepan, melt chips and peanut butter over low heat, stirring constantly until smooth. Pour over marshmallows and nuts. Let stand for 8-10 minutes. Gently stir to coat marshmallows. Chill until set; cut into bars. **Yield:** 2-1/2 dozen.

## Coconut Chip Nut Bars

Judith Strohmeyer, Albrightsville, Pennsylvania

There's something for everyone in these delectable bars, from coconut and chocolate chips to walnuts and toffee. They're popular with kids and adults alike so make a big batch. You'll be amazed at how fast they vanish!

```
1-3/4   cups all-purpose flour
  3/4   cup confectioners' sugar
  1/4   cup baking cocoa
1-1/4   cups cold butter, cubed
    1   can (14 ounces) sweetened condensed milk
    2   cups (12 ounces) semisweet chocolate chips,
        divided
    1   teaspoon vanilla extract
    1   cup chopped walnuts
  1/2   cup flaked coconut
  1/2   cup English toffee bits or almond brickle chips
```

In a small bowl, combine the flour, sugar and cocoa. Cut in butter until mixture resembles coarse crumbs. Press firmly into a greased 13-in. x 9-in. x 2-in. baking pan. Bake at 350° for 10 minutes.

Meanwhile, in a small saucepan, combine milk and 1 cup chocolate chips; cook and stir over low heat until smooth and chips are melted. Stir in vanilla.

Pour over crust. Sprinkle with walnuts and remaining chocolate chips. Top with coconut and toffee bits. Gently press down into chocolate layer. Bake at 350° for 18-20 minutes or until firm. Cool on a wire rack. Cut into bars. **Yield:** 3 dozen.

## Dream Bars

Hillary Lawson, Plummer, Idaho

These bar cookies are a family favorite and excellent travelers. Wonderfully moist and chewy, they're definite winners with all who try them.

```
CRUST:
    1   cup all-purpose flour
  1/2   cup packed brown sugar
  1/2   cup butter, cubed
FILLING:
    2   eggs, lightly beaten
    1   cup packed brown sugar
    1   teaspoon vanilla extract
    2   tablespoons all-purpose flour
  1/2   teaspoon salt
    1   cup flaked coconut
    1   cup chopped walnuts
```

In a small bowl, combine flour and brown sugar; cut in butter until crumbly. Pat into a 13-in. x 9-in. x 2-in. baking pan. Bake at 350° for 10 minutes.

Meanwhile, in a mixing bowl, beat eggs and brown sugar; stir in vanilla. Combine flour and salt; add to egg mixture. Fold in coconut and walnuts. Spread over baked crust. Return to oven and bake 20-25 minutes longer or until golden brown. Cool in pan on a wire rack. **Yield:** 32 servings.

cranberry walnut bars

## Cranberry Walnut Bars

Sylvia Gidwani, Milford, New Jersey

Perfect for autumn, the recipe for these cranberry delights was given to me by a friend. My family enjoys the bars as is or topped with ice cream.

```
  1/4   cup butter, softened
  1/2   cup sugar
  1/2   cup packed brown sugar
    1   egg
    1   teaspoon vanilla extract
1-1/4   cups all-purpose flour
    1   teaspoon baking powder
  1/4   teaspoon salt
  1/4   teaspoon ground cinnamon
    1   cup chopped fresh or frozen cranberries
  1/2   cup chopped walnuts
```

In a large mixing bowl, cream butter and sugars until light and fluffy. Beat in egg and vanilla. Combine the flour, baking powder, salt and cinnamon; gradually add to creamed mixture. Fold in cranberries and walnuts.

Spread into a greased 9-in. square baking pan. Bake at 350° for 30-35 minutes or until a toothpick inserted near the center comes out clean. Cool on a wire rack. Cut into bars. **Yield:** 1-1/2 dozen.

## Brownie Point

If you don't have the berries that are called for in Cranberry Walnut Bars, feel free to substitute them with a cup of fresh blueberries or even red currants. The walnuts can be swapped out with pecans.

chocolate caramel bars

## Chocolate Caramel Bars

Betty Hagerty, Philadelphia, Pennsylvania

These gooey bars are my most-requested treats. They're popular at school functions, family barbecues and picnics. We like them alone or topped off with a scoop of vanilla ice cream.

       2-1/4   cups all-purpose flour, *divided*
           2   cups quick-cooking oats
       1-1/2   cups packed brown sugar
           1   teaspoon baking soda
         1/2   teaspoon salt
       1-1/2   cups cold butter, cubed
           2   cups (12 ounces) semisweet chocolate chips
           1   cup chopped pecans
           1   jar (12 ounces) caramel ice cream topping

In a large bowl, combine 2 cups flour, oats, brown sugar, baking soda and salt. Cut in butter until crumbly. Set half aside for topping.

Press the remaining crumb mixture into a greased 13-in. x 9-in. x 2-in. baking pan. Bake at 350° for 15 minutes. Sprinkle with the chocolate chips and pecans.

Whisk caramel topping and remaining flour until smooth; drizzle over top. Sprinkle with the reserved crumb mixture. Bake for 18-20 minutes or until golden brown. Cool on a wire rack for 2 hours before cutting. **Yield:** about 4-1/2 dozen.

## Windmill Cookie Bars

Edna Hoffman, Hebron, Indiana

When I went to my grandma's house as a child, she was often baking Dutch windmill cookies. Like her cookies, my bars feature crisp slivered almonds.

           1   cup butter, softened
           1   cup sugar
           1   egg, *separated*
           2   cups all-purpose flour
           1   teaspoon ground cinnamon
         1/4   teaspoon baking soda
           1   cup slivered almonds

In a large mixing bowl, cream butter and sugar until light and fluffy. Beat in egg yolk. Combine the flour, cinnamon and baking soda; gradually add to creamed mixture.

Press into a greased 15-in. x 10-in. x 1-in. baking pan. Beat the egg white; brush over the dough. Sprinkle with almonds.

Bake at 350° for 20-25 minutes or until a toothpick inserted near the center comes out clean. Cool on a wire rack for 5 minutes; cut into bars. Cool completely. **Yield:** 2-1/2 dozen.

## Caramel Brownies

Clara Bakke, Coon Rapids, Minnesota

These rich, chewy brownies are full of caramel, chocolate chips and walnuts.

           2   cups sugar
         3/4   cup baking cocoa
           1   cup vegetable oil
           4   eggs
         1/4   cup milk
       1-1/2   cups all-purpose flour
           1   teaspoon salt
           1   teaspoon baking powder
           1   cup (6 ounces) semisweet chocolate chips
           1   cup chopped walnuts, *divided*
           1   package (14 ounces) caramels
           1   can (14 ounces) sweetened condensed milk

In a large mixing bowl, combine the sugar, cocoa, oil, eggs and milk. Combine the flour, salt and baking powder; add to egg mixture and mix until combined. Fold in chocolate chips and 1/2 cup walnuts.

Spoon two-thirds of the batter into a greased 13-in. x 9-in. x 2-in. baking pan. Bake at 350° for 12 minutes.

Meanwhile, in a large saucepan, heat the caramels and condensed milk over low heat until caramels are melted. Pour over baked brownie layer. Sprinkle with remaining walnuts.

Drop remaining batter by teaspoonfuls over caramel layer; carefully swirl brownie batter with a knife. Bake 35-40 minutes longer or until a toothpick inserted near the center comes out with moist crumbs. Cool on a wire rack. **Yield:** 2 dozen.

caramel brownies

hazelnut brownies

## Pecan Cream Cheese Squares

Dorothy Pritchett, Wills Point, Texas

Here's a rich and easy dessert that is perfect after a light meal. They also make good late-night treats.

- 1 package (18-1/4 ounces) yellow cake mix
- 3 eggs
- 1/2 cup butter, softened
- 2 cups chopped pecans
- 1 package (8 ounces) cream cheese, softened
- 3-2/3 cups confectioners' sugar

In a large mixing bowl, beat the cake mix, 1 egg and butter until blended. Stir in pecans. Press into a greased 13-in. x 9-in. x 2-in. baking pan; set aside.

In a small mixing bowl, beat the cream cheese, sugar and remaining eggs until smooth. Pour over pecan mixture.

Bake at 350° for 45-55 minutes or until golden brown. Cool on a wire rack; cut into squares. Store in the refrigerator. **Yield:** 3 dozen.

## Hazelnut Brownies

Becki Strader, Kennewick, Washington

I created these frosted brownies by combining several recipes. After they cooled, I divided them up and put them in the freezer or we would have eaten the entire pan! They're now a family favorite.

- 1 cup butter, melted
- 2 cups sugar
- 2 teaspoons vanilla extract
- 4 eggs
- 1 cup all-purpose flour
- 3/4 cup baking cocoa
- 1/2 teaspoon baking powder
- 1/4 teaspoon salt
- 1/2 cup chopped hazelnuts

FROSTING:
- 2 cups (12 ounces) semisweet chocolate chips
- 1 cup heavy whipping cream or refrigerated hazelnut nondairy creamer
- 2 tablespoons butter
- 1/2 cup coarsely chopped hazelnuts

In a large mixing bowl, combine the butter, sugar and vanilla until smooth. Add eggs, one at a time, beating well after each addition. Combine the flour, cocoa, baking powder and salt; gradually add to butter mixture. Fold in hazelnuts.

Spread into a greased 13-in. x 9-in. x 2-in. baking pan. Bake at 350° for 30-35 minutes or until a toothpick inserted near the center comes out clean. Cool on a wire rack.

For frosting, in a microwave, melt chips and cream until chips are melted; stir until smooth. Stir in butter until melted. Cover and refrigerate for 30 minutes or until frosting achieves spreading consistency, stirring several times. Frost brownies. Sprinkle with hazelnuts. **Yield:** 2 dozen.

## Chocolate Chip Oat Bars

Kim Wills, Sagamore Hills, Ohio

Loaded with nuts and chocolate chips, these from-scratch oat squares make a chewy addition to any snack time.

- 1 cup all-purpose flour
- 1 cup quick-cooking oats
- 3/4 cup packed brown sugar
- 1/2 cup cold butter, cubed
- 1 can (14 ounces) sweetened condensed milk
- 1 cup chopped pecans
- 1 cup (6 ounces) semisweet chocolate chips

In a large bowl, combine the flour, oats and brown sugar. Cut in the butter until crumbly. Press half of the mixture into a greased 13-in. x 9-in. x 2-in. baking pan.

Bake at 350° for 8-10 minutes. Spread condensed milk evenly over the crust. Sprinkle with pecans and chocolate chips. Top with remaining oat mixture and pat lightly. Bake for 25-30 minutes longer or until lightly browned. Cool on a wire rack. **Yield:** about 2-1/2 dozen.

chocolate chip oat bars

## Almond Coconut Brownies

Wendy Wilkins, Prattville, Alabama

I combined a couple of my favorite brownie recipes and came up with this version. My family has always enjoyed brownies and this has become a special treat.

| | |
|---|---|
| 1-1/2 | cups butter |
| 4 | squares (1 ounce *each*) unsweetened chocolate |
| 2-1/4 | cups sugar |
| 3 | eggs, lightly beaten |
| 1 | cup all-purpose flour |
| 3/4 | cup chopped slivered almonds |
| 1 | teaspoon vanilla extract |

**FILLING:**

| | |
|---|---|
| 1 | cup sugar |
| 1 | cup milk |
| 24 | large marshmallows |
| 1 | package (14 ounces) flaked coconut |

**TOPPING:**

| | |
|---|---|
| 1 | cup (6 ounces) semisweet chocolate chips |
| 3/4 | cup sugar |
| 1/4 | cup butter |
| 1/4 | cup milk |
| 1/4 | cup chopped slivered almonds, toasted |

In a microwave, melt butter and chocolate; stir until smooth. Cool slightly. Add sugar. Stir in the eggs, flour, almonds and vanilla.

Transfer to a greased 13-in. x 9-in. x 2-in. baking pan. Bake at 350° for 30 minutes or until a toothpick inserted in the center comes out clean. Cool on a wire rack.

In a large saucepan, combine filling ingredients; bring to a boil. Pour over cooled brownies.

In another saucepan, combine the chocolate chips, sugar, butter and milk; bring to a boil. Spoon over the filling. Sprinkle with almonds. Cover and refrigerate for 2 hours or until set. Store in the refrigerator. **Yield:** 4 dozen.

salted nut squares

## Salted Nut Squares

Kathy Tremel, Earling, Iowa

A favorite of young and old, this recipe came from my sister-in-law. It's simple to prepare and delicious. There's no need to keep the squares warm or cold, so they are the perfect contribution to events you have to travel to.

| | |
|---|---|
| 3 | cups salted peanuts without skins, *divided* |
| 2-1/2 | tablespoons butter |
| 2 | cups peanut butter chips |
| 1 | can (14 ounces) sweetened condensed milk |
| 2 | cups miniature marshmallows |

Place half of the peanuts in an ungreased 11-in. x 7-in. x 2-in. baking pan; set aside. In a large saucepan, melt butter and peanut butter chips over low heat; stir until smooth. Remove from the heat. Add milk and marshmallows; stir until melted.

Pour over peanuts. Sprinkle the remaining peanuts. Cover and refrigerate until chilled. Cut into bars. **Yield:** 30 servings.

almond coconut brownies

# Brownie Point

If your family members love the crunchy addition of nuts in brownies, bars or even cookies, but someone is allergic to them, try adding granola or crisp rice cereal in the same amounts as the nuts called for in your recipes.

## Butterscotch Bars

Romagene Deuel, Clarkston, Michigan

I put three recipes together to make these layered bars. I think they really satisfy the sweet tooth, and I hope you and your family do, too.

- 1 cup butter-flavored shortening
- 1 cup sugar
- 1 cup packed brown sugar
- 2 eggs
- 1 teaspoon vanilla extract
- 2 cups all-purpose flour
- 1 cup old-fashioned oats
- 1/2 teaspoon baking soda
- 1 package (10 ounces) butterscotch chips
- 1 cup chopped pecans

FILLING:
- 1 package (3 ounces) cream cheese, softened
- 2 tablespoons butter, softened
- 1/4 cup sugar
- 1 egg
- 1 tablespoon all-purpose flour

In a large mixing bowl, cream the shortening and sugars until light and fluffy. Add eggs, one at a time, beating well after each addition. Beat in vanilla.

Combine flour, oats and baking soda; gradually add to the creamed mixture. Stir in chips and pecans. Reserve 2 cups. Spread remaining dough into a greased 13-in. x 9-in. x 2-in. baking pan.

In a small mixing bowl, combine filling ingredients; beat until smooth. Spread evenly over crust. Crumble reserved dough over filling.

Bake at 375° for 40-42 minutes or until golden brown. Cool on a wire rack. Cut into bars. Store in the refrigerator. **Yield:** about 1-1/2 dozen.

## Almond Macaroon Brownies

Jayme Goffin, Crown Point, Indiana

Even when we were in the middle of remodeling our old farmhouse, I made time to bake at least three days a week. This recipe is for a slightly fancier brownie that is great for guests.

- 6 squares (1 ounce *each*) semisweet chocolate
- 1/2 cup butter
- 2/3 cup sugar
- 2 eggs
- 1 teaspoon vanilla extract
- 1 cup all-purpose flour
- 1/3 cup chopped almonds

TOPPING:
- 1 package (3 ounces) cream cheese, softened
- 1/3 cup sugar
- 1 egg
- 1 tablespoon all-purpose flour
- 1 cup flaked coconut
- 1/3 cup chopped almonds
- 16 whole almonds
- 1 square (1 ounce) semisweet chocolate, melted

In a microwave-safe bowl, melt chocolate and butter. Whisk in sugar, eggs and vanilla until smooth. Add flour and chopped almonds. Spread into a greased 8-in. square baking pan.

In a large mixing bowl, beat the cream cheese, sugar, egg and flour until smooth. Stir in coconut and chopped almonds. Spread over brownie layer. Evenly place whole almonds over topping.

Bake at 350° for 35-40 minutes until a toothpick inserted near the center comes out with moist crumbs (do not overbake). Cool on a wire rack. Drizzle with melted chocolate. **Yield:** 16 brownies.

## Chewy Peanut Butter Bars

Mrs. Sanford Wickham, Holbrook, Nebraska

This recipe features three of my favorite foods—peanut butter, coconut and chocolate—and blends them into one mouth-watering dessert. It's very rich and filling, so a small piece is usually enough.

- 1 cup all-purpose flour
- 1/3 cup sugar
- 1/2 cup butter

FILLING:
- 2 eggs
- 1/2 cup corn syrup
- 1/2 cup sugar
- 1/4 cup crunchy peanut butter
- 1/4 teaspoon salt
- 1/2 cup flaked coconut
- 1/2 cup semisweet chocolate chips

In a bowl, combine flour and sugar; cut in the butter until mixture is crumbly. Press into a greased 13-in. x 9-in. x 2-in. baking pan. Bake at 350° for 14-16 minutes or until lightly browned.

In a large mixing bowl, beat the eggs, corn syrup, sugar, peanut butter and salt until smooth. Fold in coconut and chocolate chips. Pour over crust. Return to the oven for 15-20 minutes or until golden. Cool on a wire rack. Cut into bars. **Yield:** 3 dozen.

chewy peanut butter bars

# Chapter 5

p. 70

p. 74

p. 77

p. 78

p. 79

# Frosted Brownies

These snackable sensations are the icing on the cake—or should we say on the brownie? Classic glazes and creamy frostings spell sweet success for these delectable gems.

mocha mousse brownies

## Mocha Mousse Brownies

Stacy Waller, Eagan, Minnesota

Chocolate is one of my favorite foods, and these dark chocolate goodies are the perfect pairing of coffee-flavored mousse and fudge brownie. My friends and family just love them.

- 2/3 cup semisweet chocolate chips
- 1/2 cup butter
- 1 cup plus 2 tablespoons sugar
- 2 eggs
- 1/4 cup hot water
- 2 tablespoons instant coffee granules
- 1/2 cup all-purpose flour
- 1/2 cup baking cocoa
- 1 teaspoon baking powder

MOCHA MOUSSE:
- 1 package (3 ounces) cream cheese, softened
- 1/4 cup sweetened condensed milk
- 1/2 cup semisweet chocolate chips, melted
- 1 envelope unflavored gelatin
- 1/4 cup cold water
- 2 tablespoons instant coffee granules
- 1 cup heavy whipping cream

In a saucepan over low heat, melt the chips and butter; pour into a mixing bowl. Beat in sugar until smooth. Add eggs, one at a time, beating well after each addition. Combine hot water and coffee granules; add to chocolate mixture. Combine the flour, cocoa and baking powder; gradually beat into chocolate mixture.

Spread into a greased 13-in. x 9-in. x 2-in. baking pan. Bake at 350° for 15-20 minutes or until a toothpick inserted near the center comes out clean (brownies will be thin). Cool on a wire rack.

For mousse, in a small mixing bowl, beat cream cheese until smooth; beat in milk and melted chips. In a small saucepan, sprinkle gelatin over cold water; let stand for 1 minute. Cook and stir over low heat until gelatin is dissolved. Remove from the heat; stir in coffee granules until dissolved. In a small mixing bowl, beat whipping cream until slightly thickened. Beat in gela-

tin. Fold into cream cheese mixture. Spread over brownies. Cover and refrigerate for 3 hours or until firm. Cut into squares. **Yield:** 2 dozen.

## Double-Decker Brownies

Heather Hooker, Belmont, Ontario

With two taste-tempting layers and a butterscotch frosting, no one will be able to eat just one of these brownies!

CHOCOLATE LAYER:
- 2 eggs, lightly beaten
- 1 cup sugar
- 3/4 cup all-purpose flour
- 1/2 cup chopped walnuts
Pinch salt
- 1/2 cup butter, melted
- 1/4 cup baking cocoa

BUTTERSCOTCH LAYER:
- 1/2 cup butter, softened
- 1-1/2 cups packed brown sugar
- 2 eggs
- 2 teaspoons vanilla extract
- 1-1/2 cups all-purpose flour
- 1/4 teaspoon salt
- 1/2 cup chopped walnuts

FROSTING:
- 1/4 cup butter, cubed
- 1/2 cup packed brown sugar
- 3 tablespoons milk
- 1-1/2 cups confectioners' sugar, sifted
- 1/3 cup semisweet chocolate chips
- 1/3 cup butterscotch chips
- 1 tablespoon shortening

double-decker brownies

frosted cake brownies

In a large bowl, combine the eggs, sugar, flour, walnuts and salt. In another bowl, stir butter and cocoa until smooth; stir into to egg mixture until blended. Pour into a greased 13-in. x 9-in. x 2-in. baking pan; set aside.

For butterscotch layer, in a large mixing bowl, cream butter and brown sugar until light and fluffy. Beat in eggs and vanilla. Stir in the flour, salt and walnuts.

Spoon over chocolate layer. Bake at 350° for 30-35 minutes or until brownies begin to pull away from sides of pan. Cool on a wire rack.

For frosting, in a small saucepan, combine the butter, brown sugar and milk; bring to a boil and boil for 2 minutes. Remove from the heat; stir in confectioners' sugar until smooth. Quickly spread over brownies.

In a microwave, melt chocolate chips, butterscotch chips and shortening; stir until smooth. Drizzle over frosting. **Yield:** 3 dozen.

## Frosted Cake Brownies

Mary Fox, Forest City, Iowa

A boxed mix is the base for these moist brownies with from-scratch taste. It uses about half of a can of prepared frosting. Save the rest, because you'll make them again.

  1   package fudge brownie mix (13-inch x 9-inch pan size)
  1   cup (8 ounces) sour cream
  1   cup milk chocolate chips
1/2  cup chopped walnuts
  1   cup milk chocolate frosting

Prepare brownie mix according to package directions. Fold in the sour cream, chocolate chips and walnuts into batter.

Pour into a greased 13-in. x 9-in. x 2-in. baking pan. Bake at 350° for 30-35 minutes or until a toothpick inserted near the center comes out clean. Cool completely on a wire rack. Frost. Cut into bars. **Yield:** 2-1/2 dozen.

## Choco-Cloud Brownies

Linda Roecker, Hazelton, North Dakota

True to its name, this mild chocolate treat is covered by a cloud of light fluffy frosting. My husband and I have three young daughters who like to bake them as much as I do.

  1   cup butter, softened
  2   cups sugar
  4   eggs
  1   milk chocolate candy bar (7 ounces), melted
  3   teaspoons vanilla extract
  2   cups all-purpose flour
1/2  teaspoon salt
  2   cups chopped pecans
**FROSTING:**
  5   tablespoons all-purpose flour
  1   cup milk
  1   cup butter, softened
  1   cup confectioners' sugar
  2   teaspoons vanilla extract
**Baking cocoa**

In a large mixing bowl, cream butter and sugar until light and fluffy. Add eggs, one at a time, beating well after each. Beat in chocolate and vanilla. Gradually add flour and salt. Stir in pecans.

Spread into a greased 13-in. x 9-in. x 2-in. baking pan. Bake at 350° for 35-40 minutes or until center is set and edges pull away from pan. Cool on a wire rack.

For frosting, in a small saucepan, combine flour and milk. Bring to a boil; cook and stir for 2 minutes or until thickened. Cool completely.

In a small mixing bowl, cream butter and confectioners' sugar until light and fluffy. Beat in vanilla. Gradually add milk mixture; beat for 5 minutes or until fluffy. Frost brownies; dust with cocoa. Cut into bars. Store in the refrigerator. **Yield:** about 2-1/2 dozen.

choco-cloud brownies

# Cute Creations

Cookie cutters, colored glaze and a good imagination are all you need to jazz up brownies and bars. Ideal for birthday parties and school treats, consider these four fun and easy ideas.

zebra sweets

## Football Brownies

Taste of Home Test Kitchen

Homemade chocolate frosting adds a special touch to these sporting brownies prepared from a mix.

- 1 package fudge brownie mix (13-inch x 9-inch pan size)
- 6 tablespoons butter, softened
- 2-3/4 cups confectioners' sugar
- 1/2 cup baking cocoa
- 1/3 cup milk
- 1 teaspoon vanilla extract
- 1/4 cup vanilla *or* white chips

Prepare the brownie batter according to package directions. Spread into a greased 15-in. x 10-in. x 1-in. baking pan. Bake at 350° for 13-15 minutes or until a toothpick comes out clean. Cool on a wire rack.

In a large mixing bowl, beat the butter, sugar, cocoa, milk and vanilla until smooth. Frost the cooled brownies. Loosely cover and chill for 1 hour or until the frosting is set.

With a sharp knife, make 1-1/2-in. parallel cuts from a short side to a long side to form diamonds. In a microwave, melt vanilla chips at 50% power; stir until smooth. Place in a small heavy-duty resealable plastic bag; cut a small hole in a corner of bag. Pipe laces on brownies. **Yield:** about 3 dozen.

## Zebra Sweets

Taste of Home Test Kitchen

A horse-shaped cookie cutter is the key to these tasty treats made with marshmallow and crisp rice cereal. Melted vanilla and chocolate chips create the zebra's eye-catching stripes.

- 8 cups miniature marshmallows
- 6 tablespoons butter, cubed
- 12 cups crisp rice cereal
- 1 cup vanilla chips
- 1 teaspoon shortening, *divided*
- 1 cup (6 ounces) semisweet chocolate chips

In a large saucepan, heat marshmallows and butter until almost melted. Remove from the heat. Stir in cereal; toss to coat. Press firmly into a greased 15-in. x 10-in x. 1-in. baking pan. Cut with a horse-shaped cookie cutter. Remove cutouts to waxed paper; set aside.

In a microwave, melt vanilla chips and 1/2 teaspoon shortening; stir until smooth. Spread over cutouts. Let dry on waxed paper.

In a microwave, melt chocolate chips and remaining shortening; stir until smooth. Place in a heavy-duty plastic bag. Cut a small hole in the corner of the bag; pipe mane, stripes, hooves, etc. on zebras. **Yield:** about 1 dozen.

football brownies

## Witch Hat Treats

Nancy Foust, Stoneboro, Pennsylvania

Here's a clever twist on ordinary marshmallow cereal treats. They add a festive touch to Halloween.

      3  tablespoons butter
      1  package (10 ounces) large marshmallows
    1/2  cup peanut butter
      6  cups crisp rice cereal
  1-1/2  cups milk chocolate chips
      1  teaspoon shortening
Orange frosting
Chocolate jimmies
Rope black licorice

In a large microwave-safe bowl, melt butter on high for about 30 seconds. Add marshmallows; stir to coat. Microwave on high 30-40 seconds longer or until smooth. Stir in peanut butter. Immediately add cereal; stir gently until coated. Press into a greased 13-in. x 9-in. x 2-in. pan.

In a small microwave-safe bowl, heat chocolate chips and shortening on 70% power for 45 seconds. Heat in 10 to 20 second intervals until melted; stir until smooth. Spread over cereal mixture. Cool completely.

Cut into 2-1/2-in. x 2-in. triangles, with a thin base on bottom of triangle for hat brim. Decorate with frosting, jimmies for the buckle and licorice for the brim. **Yield:** 2 dozen.

***Editor's Note:*** *This recipe was tested in a 1,100-watt microwave.*

witch hat treats

jack-o'-lantern brownies

## Jack-o'-Lantern Brownies

Flo Burtnett, Gage, Oklahoma

Hosting a Halloween party? Use a cookie cutter to easily cut these from-scratch chocolate brownies into pumpkin shapes, then give them personality with orange, black and green frosting. Our grandchildren think these are great.

    3/4  cup butter, melted
  1-1/2  cups sugar
  1-1/2  teaspoons vanilla extract
      3  eggs
    3/4  cup all-purpose flour
    1/2  cup baking cocoa
    1/2  teaspoon baking powder
    1/4  teaspoon salt
      1  can (16 ounces) vanilla frosting
Orange paste food coloring
Green and black decorating gel
Candy corn and milk chocolate M&M's, optional

In a large mixing bowl, cream the butter, sugar and vanilla until light and fluffy. Beat in eggs until well blended. Combine the flour, cocoa, baking powder and salt; gradually add to butter mixture.

Line a greased 13-in. x 9-in. x 2-in. baking pan with waxed paper; grease the paper. Spread batter evenly in pan. Bake at 350° for 18-22 minutes or until brownies begin to pull away from sides of pan. Cool on a wire rack.

Run a knife around edge of pan. Invert brownies onto a work surface and remove waxed paper. Cut brownies with a 3-in. pumpkin cookie cutter, leaving at least 1/8 in. between each shape. (Discard scraps or save for another use.)

Tint frosting with orange food coloring; frost brownies. Use green gel to create the pumpkin stems and black gel and candy corn and M&M's to decorate the faces if desired. **Yield:** about 1 dozen.

raspberry truffle brownies

## Raspberry Truffle Brownies

Leslie Knicl, Mahomet, Illinois

On the outside, these look like traditional brownies. When people bite in, though, are they surprised! It's almost like eating a rich, fudge-filled chocolate candy.

- 1/2 cup butter, cubed
- 1-1/4 cups semisweet chocolate chips
- 2 eggs
- 3/4 cup packed brown sugar
- 1 teaspoon instant coffee granules
- 2 tablespoons water
- 3/4 cup all-purpose flour
- 1/2 teaspoon baking powder

FILLING:
- 1 cup (6 ounces) semisweet chocolate chips
- 1 package (8 ounces) cream cheese, softened
- 1/4 cup confectioners' sugar
- 1/3 cup seedless red raspberry jam

GLAZE:
- 1/4 cup semisweet chocolate chips
- 1 teaspoon shortening

In a heavy saucepan, melt butter and chocolate chips over low heat. Cool slightly. In a large bowl, beat eggs and brown sugar. Dissolve coffee crystals in water; add to egg mixture with melted chocolate. Mix well. Combine the flour and baking powder; stir into the chocolate mixture.

Spread in a greased 9-in. square baking pan. Bake at 350° for 30-35 minutes or until brownies test done. Cool on a wire rack.

For filling, melt chocolate chips; cool. In a small mixing bowl, beat cream cheese and confectioners' sugar until smooth. Beat in jam. Stir in melted chocolate; spread over cooled brownies.

For glaze, melt chocolate chips and shortening. Drizzle over filling. Chill before cutting. Store in the refrigerator. **Yield:** about 5 dozen.

## Teddy Carrot Bars

Susan Schuller, Brainerd, Minnesota

At a baby shower, I was sure to point out to the mother-to-be and guests that these yummy bars include two jars of baby food! Decorating them with purchased Teddy Grahams took little time and conveniently carried out the baby-shower theme.

- 1-1/4 cups all-purpose flour
- 1 cup sugar
- 1 teaspoon baking soda
- 1 teaspoon ground cinnamon
- 1/2 teaspoon salt
- 1 jar (6 ounces) carrot baby food
- 1 jar (6 ounces) applesauce baby food
- 2 eggs
- 2 tablespoons vegetable oil

CREAM CHEESE FROSTING:
- 1 package (3 ounces) cream cheese, softened
- 1 teaspoon vanilla extract
- 2 to 2-1/2 cups confectioners' sugar
- 1 to 3 teaspoons milk
- 24 cinnamon-flavored bear-shaped graham crackers

In a large bowl, combine flour, sugar, baking soda, cinnamon and salt. In a small bowl, combine the baby foods, eggs and oil; add to dry ingredients just until blended.

Pour into a greased 13-in. x 9-in. x 2-in. baking pan. Bake at 350° for 20-25 minutes or until a toothpick inserted near the center comes out clean. Cool completely on a wire rack. Cut into bars.

For frosting, in a large mixing bowl, beat cream cheese and vanilla until smooth. Gradually add confectioners' sugar. Add enough to milk to achieve desired consistency. Place a dollop of frosting on each bar; top with a bear-shaped graham cracker. **Yield:** 2 dozen.

teddy carrot bars

microwave oatmeal bars

## Microwave Oatmeal Bars

Annette Self, Junction City, Ohio

You only need five ingredients for these change-of-pace bars. Try them in the autumn with cups of hot coffee.

- 2 cups quick-cooking oats
- 1/2 cup packed brown sugar
- 1/2 cup butter, melted
- 1/4 cup corn syrup
- 1 cup (6 ounces) semisweet chocolate chips

In a bowl, combine oats and brown sugar. Stir in butter and corn syrup. Press into a greased 9-in. square microwave-safe dish. Microwave, uncovered, on high for 1-1/2 minutes. Rotate a half turn; microwave 1-1/2 minutes longer. Sprinkle with chocolate chips. Microwave at 30% power for 4-1/2 minutes or until chips are glossy; spread chocolate evenly over top. Refrigerate 15-20 minutes before cutting. **Yield:** 8-10 servings.

*Editor's Note: This recipe was tested in a 1,100-watt microwave.*

## Spice Cake Bars

Dena Hayden, Vassar, Michigan

Whenever I went to Grandmother's, she served these flavorful bars topped with creamy frosting. Today, I do the same for our grandchildren, who like the little treats just as much.

- 1 cup butter, softened
- 1 cup sugar
- 1 cup molasses
- 1 cup hot water
- 1 egg
- 3 cups all-purpose flour
- 2 teaspoons ground ginger
- 2 teaspoons ground allspice
- 1 teaspoon baking soda
- 1 teaspoon ground cloves

FROSTING:
- 1/2 cup shortening
- 1/2 cup butter, softened

- 2 to 3 teaspoons lemon juice
- 4 cups confectioners' sugar

In a large mixing bowl, cream butter and sugar until fluffy. Beat in the molasses, water and egg. Combine flour, ginger, allspice, baking soda and cloves; gradually add to the creamed mixture. Pour into a greased 15-in. x 10-in. x 1-in. baking pan.

Bake at 375° for 18-22 minutes or until a toothpick inserted near the center comes out clean. Cool on wire rack. Meanwhile, in a small mixing bowl, beat shortening, butter and lemon juice until smooth. Beat in sugar until light and fluffy. Frost bars. **Yield:** about 2 dozen.

## Black 'n' White Brownies

Laurie Knoke, DeKalb, Illinois

The extra effort it takes to make these layered brownies is worthwhile. My mother won a prize for the recipe.

- 3/4 cup all-purpose flour
- 1/2 cup sugar
- 1/4 teaspoon baking powder
- 1/4 teaspoon salt
- 1 cup quick-cooking oats
- 1 cup flaked coconut
- 2/3 cup butter, melted
- 2 tablespoons milk

CHOCOLATE LAYER:
- 1/3 cup butter
- 1 square (1 ounce) unsweetened chocolate
- 2 eggs
- 1 cup packed brown sugar
- 2 tablespoons milk
- 1 teaspoon vanilla extract
- 3/4 cup all-purpose flour
- 1/2 teaspoon baking powder
- 1/4 teaspoon salt
- 1/2 cup chopped walnuts

FROSTING:
- 4 ounces cream cheese, softened
- 1/4 cup butter, softened
- 1-1/2 teaspoons vanilla extract
- 2-1/4 cups confectioners' sugar
- 1/4 cup chopped walnuts

In a large bowl, combine the first four ingredients. Stir in oats and coconut. Add butter and milk. Press into a greased 13-in. x 9-in. x 2-in. baking pan. Bake at 350° for 10-12 minutes. Remove from the oven. Reduce heat to 325°.

In a small saucepan, melt the butter and chocolate; cool slightly. In a large mixing bowl, beat the eggs, brown sugar, milk and vanilla until well blended. Beat in the chocolate mixture. Combine the flour, baking powder and salt; gradually add to chocolate mixture. Stir in walnuts. Spread evenly over crust.

Bake at 325° for 25-30 minutes or until a toothpick comes out with moist crumbs (do not overbake). Cool on a wire rack.

In a small mixing bowl, combine the first four frosting ingredients until smooth and creamy. Spread over bars. Sprinkle with walnuts. Store in the refrigerator. **Yield:** 4 dozen.

## Double Frosted Brownies

Jean Kolessar, Orland Park, Illinois

For a quick dessert or bake sale contribution, this recipe is ideal. A packaged brownie mix is dressed up with two kinds of frosting, creating a two-toned treat with a luscious look and sweet taste.

- 1 package fudge brownie mix (13-inch x 9-inch pan size)
- 1/2 cup butter, softened
- 1-1/2 cups confectioners' sugar
- 2 tablespoons instant vanilla pudding mix
- 2 to 3 tablespoons milk
- 1 can (16 ounces) chocolate fudge frosting

Prepare brownie mix according to package directions. Spread the batter into a greased 13-in. x 9-in. x 2-in. baking pan. Bake at 350° for 25-30 minutes or until a toothpick inserted 2 in. from side of pan comes out clean. Cool completely on a wire rack.

In a large mixing bowl, beat the butter, sugar and pudding mix until blended. Add enough milk to achieve spreading consistency. Frost brownies. Cover and refrigerate for 30 minutes. Spread with fudge frosting. Cut into bars. Store in the refrigerator. **Yield:** 3 dozen.

## Chocolate Raspberry Bars

Diana Olmstead, Yelm, Washington

A cake mix and raspberry jam simplify assembly of my favorite goodies. The bars are very rich, so you may want to cut them into small pieces.

- 1 package (18-1/4 ounces) devil's food cake mix
- 1 egg
- 1/3 cup butter, softened

double frosted brownies

chocolate raspberry bars

- 1 jar (12 ounces) seedless raspberry jam

TOPPING:
- 1 package (10 to 12 ounces) vanilla *or* white chips
- 1 package (8 ounces) cream cheese, softened
- 2 tablespoons milk
- 1/2 cup semisweet chocolate chips
- 2 tablespoons butter

In a large bowl, combine the dry cake mix, egg and butter until crumbly. Press into a greased 15-in. x 10-in. x 1-in. baking pan.

Bake at 350° for 8-10 minutes or until a toothpick inserted near the center comes out clean (crust will appear puffy and dry). Cool on a wire rack. Spread jam over the crust.

In a microwave, melt vanilla chips; stir until smooth. In a large mixing bowl, beat cream cheese and milk until smooth. Stir in melted chips. Carefully spread over the jam.

In a microwave, melt chocolate chips and butter; stir until smooth. Drizzle or pipe over the cream cheese layer. Refrigerate before cutting. **Yield:** about 6 dozen.

## Napoleon Cremes

Gloria Jesswein, Niles, Michigan

For the annual Christmas open house we host, I set out a buffet with lots of food and treats like these lovely layered bars. They're so creamy...and with a green pistachio layer of pudding peeking out, they're very merry.

- 1 cup butter, softened, *divided*
- 1/4 cup sugar
- 1/4 cup baking cocoa
- 1 teaspoon vanilla extract
- 1 egg, lightly beaten
- 2 cups finely crushed graham cracker crumbs (about 32 squares)

1 cup flaked coconut
3 tablespoons milk
1 package (3.4 ounces) instant pistachio *or* lemon pudding mix
2 cups confectioners' sugar
TOPPING:
1 cup (6 ounces) semisweet chocolate chips
3 tablespoons butter

In a large heavy saucepan, combine 1/2 cup butter, sugar, cocoa and vanilla; cook and stir until butter is melted. Add egg; cook and stir until mixture thickens, about 5 minutes. Stir in crumbs and coconut. Press into a greased 9-in. square baking pan.

In a small mixing bowl, beat remaining butter until smooth. Add milk, pudding mix and confectioners' sugar; beat until fluffy. Spread over crust. Refrigerate until firm, 1-1/2 to 2 hours.

In a microwave, melt chocolate chips and butter; stir until smooth. Cool. Spread over pudding layer. Chill until set. Cut into bars. **Yield:** 4 dozen.

## Frosted Cookie Brownies

Alicia French, Crestline, California

Years ago, my children and I came up with these bars by combining two of their favorite treats. With a crisp cookie crust and a fluffy frosting, these brownies are the most requested dessert at our house.

1 tube (18 ounces) refrigerated chocolate chip cookie dough
3 cups miniature marshmallows
2 cups (12 ounces) semisweet chocolate chips
1 cup butter, cubed
4 eggs

frosted cookie brownies

2 teaspoons vanilla extract
1 cup all-purpose flour
1/2 teaspoon baking powder
1/4 teaspoon salt
1 cup chopped walnuts
FROSTING:
2 cups miniature marshmallows
6 tablespoons milk
1/4 cup butter, softened
2 squares (1 ounce *each*) unsweetened chocolate
3 cups confectioners' sugar

Press cookie dough into a greased 13-in. x 9-in. x 2-in. baking pan. Bake at 350° for 10 minutes.

Meanwhile, in a large saucepan, combine the marshmallows, chips and butter; cook and stir over low heat until melted and smooth. Transfer to a large mixing bowl; cool. Beat in eggs and vanilla. Combine the flour, baking powder and salt; stir into marshmallow mixture. Stir in nuts.

Spread over cookie crust. Bake for 30-35 minutes or until a toothpick inserted near the center comes out clean. Cool on a wire rack.

For frosting, in a small saucepan, combine the marshmallows, milk, butter and chocolate. Cook and stir over low heat until smooth. Remove from the heat; beat in confectioners' sugar until smooth. Frost brownies. Cut into bars. **Yield:** 15 servings.

napoleon cremes

## Brownie Point

Slice through a pan of brownies with ease by using a pizza cutter treated with nonstick cooking spray.

## Double Brownies

Rosanne Stevenson, Melfort, Saskatchewan

Between farm chores, gardening and taking the kids to their many activities, I manage to keep quite busy. I do, however, like to bake, and these caramel-iced treats appear on our menu quite often.

**BOTTOM LAYER:**
| | |
|---|---|
| 1/2 | cup butter, softened |
| 1-1/4 | cups packed brown sugar |
| 2 | eggs |
| 2 | teaspoons vanilla extract |
| 1-1/2 | cups all-purpose flour |
| 1/4 | teaspoon salt |
| 1/2 | cup chopped walnuts |

**MIDDLE LAYER:**
| | |
|---|---|
| 1/2 | cup butter, softened |
| 1 | cup sugar |
| 2 | eggs |
| 3/4 | cup all-purpose flour |
| 1/4 | cup baking cocoa |
| 1/8 | teaspoon salt |
| 1/2 | cup chopped walnuts |

**CARAMEL ICING:**
| | |
|---|---|
| 6 | tablespoons butter |
| 3/4 | cup packed brown sugar |
| 4 | to 6 tablespoons milk |
| 2-1/2 | cups confectioners' sugar |

In a large mixing bowl, cream the butter and brown sugar. Beat in eggs and vanilla. Combine flour and salt. Stir into creamed mixture. Stir in nuts. Spread into a greased 13-in. x 9-in. x 2-in. baking pan; set aside.

For middle layer, cream butter and sugar. Beat in eggs. Combine the flour, cocoa and salt. Stir into creamed mixture. Add nuts. Spread over the bottom layer. Bake at 350° for 30-35 minutes or until a toothpick inserted near the center comes out clean. Cool on wire rack.

For icing, melt butter in a saucepan over medium heat. Stir in brown sugar and milk; bring to a boil. Re-

double brownies

creamy cashew brownies

move from the heat. Cool just until warm; beat in confectioners' sugar until the icing achieves spreading consistency. Spread over brownies. Let stand until set. Cut into bars. **Yield:** 2 dozen.

## Creamy Cashew Brownies

Karen Wagner, Danville, Illinois

My sister-in-law dubbed me the "dessert queen" because of treats like this that I take to our family get-togethers. The brownies have a fudge-like texture and a rich cream cheese topping. Cashews and a hot fudge swirl make the pretty bars special.

| | |
|---|---|
| 1 | package fudge brownie mix (13-inch x 9-inch pan size) |
| 1/3 | cup water |
| 1/4 | cup vegetable oil |
| 1 | egg |
| 1 | cup (6 ounces) semisweet chocolate chips |

**TOPPING:**
| | |
|---|---|
| 2 | packages (8 ounces *each*) cream cheese, softened |
| 1-1/2 | cups confectioners' sugar |
| 1 | teaspoon vanilla extract |
| 1 | cup salted cashews, coarsely chopped |
| 1/2 | cup hot fudge ice cream topping, warmed |

In a large bowl, combine the brownie mix, water, oil and egg. Stir in chips. Spread into a greased 13-in. x 9-in. x 2-in. baking pan.

Bake at 350° for 25-27 minutes or until a toothpick inserted near the center comes out clean (do not overbake). Cool on a wire rack.

For topping, in a large mixing bowl, beat the cream cheese, confectioners' sugar and vanilla until smooth. Spread over brownies. Sprinkle with cashews; drizzle with hot fudge topping. Refrigerate before cutting. Store in the refrigerator. **Yield:** 2 dozen.

# Fudgy Nut Brownies

Ruth Stern, Shadow Hills, California

I've prepared this special recipe for many open house and potluck dinners. It came from an old roommate, who is now a grandmother. While in our early 20s, we never imagined we'd have fun sharing brownie recipes after all these years.

```
2-1/2   cups semisweet chocolate chips
    1   cup butter
    1   cup sugar
  1/4   teaspoon salt
    4   eggs
    2   teaspoons vanilla extract
  3/4   cup all-purpose flour
    1   cup coarsely chopped hazelnuts
```
TOPPING:
```
   12   squares (1 ounce each) semisweet chocolate
    1   tablespoon shortening
    3   squares (1 ounce each) white baking chocolate
```

In a heavy saucepan or microwave, melt chocolate chips and butter; stir until smooth. Add sugar and salt; stir until dissolved. Cool for 10 minutes. Stir in eggs, vanilla, flour and nuts.

Spread into a greased 15-in. x 10-in. x 1-in. baking pan. Bake at 350° for 25-30 minutes or until a toothpick inserted near the center comes out with moist crumbs (do not overbake). Cool completely on a wire rack.

For topping, melt semisweet chocolate and shortening in a heavy saucepan or microwave; stir until smooth. Spread over brownies. Melt white chocolate; cool slightly. Pour into a small heavy-duty resealable plastic bag; cut a small hole in corner of bag. Pipe thin lines 1 in. apart widthwise. Beginning about 1 in. from a wide side, gently pull a toothpick through the lines to

glazed mint brownies

the opposite side. Wipe toothpick clean. Then pull toothpick through lines in opposite directions. Repeat over entire top at 1-in. intervals. Cut into bars. **Yield:** about 2-1/2 dozen.

# Glazed Mint Brownies

Diana Conner, Wichita, Kansas

I love taking these rich, minty bars to ladies' luncheons. The women always think I've worked hard to make the layered brownies when they're so easy to bake!

```
    2   squares (1 ounce each) unsweetened
        chocolate
  1/2   cup butter
    2   eggs
    1   cup sugar
  1/2   cup all-purpose flour
```
FILLING:
```
    3   tablespoons butter, softened
1-1/2   cups confectioners' sugar
    2   tablespoons milk
  3/4   teaspoon peppermint extract
    3   to 4 drops green food coloring, optional
```
GLAZE:
```
  1/2   cup semisweet chocolate chips
    2   tablespoons butter
```

In a microwave, melt chocolate and butter; stir until smooth. Cool slightly. In a large mixing bowl, beat the eggs, sugar and flour until blended. Stir in the chocolate mixture.

Pour into a greased 9-in. square baking pan. Bake at 350° for 20-25 minutes or until a toothpick inserted near the center comes out clean. Cool on a wire rack.

In a small mixing bowl, beat the filling ingredients until creamy. Spread over brownies.

For glaze, in a microwave, melt chocolate chips and butter; stir until smooth. Spread over filling. Refrigerate until filling and glaze are set. **Yield:** 12-16 brownies.

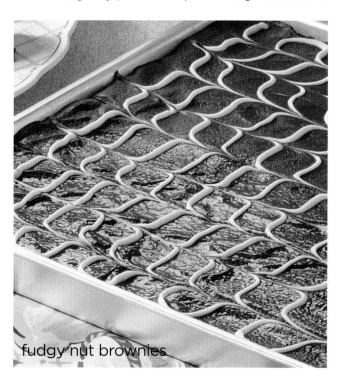

fudgy nut brownies

# Heartwarming Bites Easily Beat Winter Doldrums

Surprise your family with these cute treats and watch the kitchen light up with smiles. Perfect for formal holidays and casual get-togethers alike, they're sure to become your signature contribution.

## Valentine Brownies

Susan Ohlendorf, Austin, Texas

To show my loved ones how much they mean to me, I prepare brownies from a mix, cut a heart shape out of each one and fill the center with homemade frosting. Our grandson loves to eat the little heart-shaped brownies that are left over.

> 1 package fudge brownie mix (13-inch x 9-inch pan size)
> 1/2 cup butter, softened
> 1-1/2 cups confectioners' sugar
> 1/4 teaspoon vanilla extract
> 1/4 cup baking cocoa

valentine brownies

Prepare and bake brownie mix according to package directions for fudge-like brownies. Cool completely on a wire rack.

Meanwhile, in a small mixing bowl, cream the butter, confectioners' sugar and vanilla until light and fluffy. Place in a heavy-duty resealable plastic bag; cut a small hole in a corner of bag; set aside.

Line a baking sheet with waxed paper. Dust with cocoa; set aside. Cut brownies into 15 rectangles. Using a 1-1/2-in. heart-shaped cookie cutter, cut out a heart from the center of each brownie. Reserve cutout centers for another use. Place brownies on prepared baking sheet. Pipe frosting into centers of brownies. **Yield:** 15 brownies.

## Gift-Wrapped Brownies

Dopris Roots, Big Timber, Montana

With bright green and red frosting "ribbon" piped on top, these chocolaty "packages" are a pretty addition to any holiday gathering. They'll make a sweet gift for everyone on your Christmas list!

> 1/2 cup shortening
> 4 squares (1 ounce *each*) semisweet baking chocolate
> 3 eggs
> 1 cup sugar
> 2 teaspoons vanilla extract, *divided*
> 1/2 cup all-purpose flour
> 1/2 cup chopped nuts
> 1/2 teaspoon salt
> 1/2 teaspoon baking powder
> 2 cups confectioners' sugar
> 1/4 cup heavy whipping cream
> Red and green food coloring

In a microwave, melt shortening and chocolate; stir until smooth. Set aside. In a large mixing bowl, beat eggs, sugar and 1 teaspoon vanilla. Gradually add the flour, nuts, salt, baking powder and chocolate mixture.

Pour into a greased 8-in. square baking pan. Bake at 350° for 20-25 minutes or until a toothpick inserted near the center comes out clean. Cool on a wire rack. Cut into 2-in. x 1-in. rectangles; remove from pan.

In a large mixing bowl, beat the confectioners' sugar, cream and remaining vanilla until smooth; set half aside. Spread remaining frosting over top of brownies. Tint half of the reserved frosting red and half green.

Cut a small hole in the corner of two plastic or pastry bags; fill one bag with red frosting and one with green. Insert pastry tip if desired. To decorate, pipe ribbon and bows on brownies or create designs of your choice. **Yield:** 2-1/2 dozen.

## Ice Skate Brownies

Kathy Kittell, Lenexa, Kansas

Figure on these goodies winning lots of smiles! The graceful snacks are perfect for a wintertime birthday bash, a classroom treat or anytime you'd like to surprise your gang.

|  |  |
|--|--|
| 16 | squares (1 ounce *each*) white baking chocolate |
| 1 | cup butter |
| 1 | cup sugar |
| 4 | eggs |
| 2 | teaspoons vanilla extract |
| 1 | teaspoon salt |
| 2 | cups all-purpose flour |
| 2 | cups (12 ounces) semisweet chocolate chips |
| 2 | packages (10 to 12 ounces *each*) vanilla *or* white chips |
| 1/4 | cup plus 1/2 teaspoon shortening, *divided* |
| 34 | miniature candy canes |

**Red and blue gel food coloring**

Chop half of the white baking chocolate squares. Set chopped chocolate aside.

In a small saucepan, combine the butter and remaining white chocolate squares. Cook and stir over low heat until melted and smooth.

In a large mixing bowl, beat sugar and eggs until light and lemon-colored. Beat in the melted white chocolate, vanilla and salt. Stir in flour. Fold in 1-1/2 cups of chocolate chips and reserved chopped white chocolate.

Spoon batter into a greased 15-in. x 10-in. x 1-in. baking pan. Bake at 350° for 25-30 minutes or until a toothpick inserted near the center comes out clean. Cool on a wire rack.

Trace an ice skate pattern onto tracing paper with pencil and cut out. Trace around pattern onto cardboard and cut out for template.

Using the template and a sharp knife, cut out 34 skates from brownies, flipping the template over as desired to cut some skates in reverse. Place on a waxed paper-lined baking sheet and freeze for 15-20 minutes or until set.

Meanwhile, in a microwave-safe bowl, combine vanilla chips and 1/4 cup of shortening. Microwave at 70%

ice skate brownies

power for 1 minute. Microwave in 10-to-20 second intervals until chips are melted; stir until smooth.

Dip each brownie into melted vanilla chip mixture. Place on a waxed paper-lined baking sheet. Let stand until set.

In a microwave-safe bowl, combine remaining chocolate chips and shortening. Microwave, uncovered, on high for 1-2 minutes or until melted; stir until smooth. Spread melted chocolate over the heel of each skate.

For skate blades, use knife to trim the curved end of each candy cane. Referring to photo above for position, use remaining white chip mixture to attach a candy cane to bottom of each skate.

Referring to the photo for position, use red gel to pipe laces on skates. Use blue gel to pipe a snowflake on each. **Yield:** 34 brownies.

*Finished size: Including candy-cane blades, each brownie measures about 2-1/4 inches high x 2-3/8 inches wide.*

## Brownie Point

To give plain brownies a sensational new twist, sprinkle a layer of mint chocolate chips over the brownies as soon as you remove the pan from the oven. Once the chips melt, spread the chocolate over the brownies and allow them to cool before serving.

# Chapter 6

p. 89

p. 84

p. 89

p. 92

p. 93

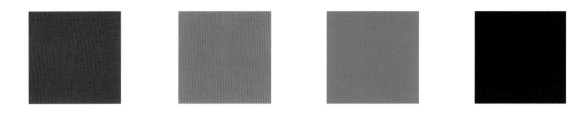

# Time-Saving Treats

When you're in need of something sweet but don't have time to spare, whip up a simply scrumptious delight with these quick-to-fix brownies and bars.

## Candy Cereal Treats

Janet Shearer, Jackson, Michigan

These scrumptious bars travel well and are loved by kids of all ages.

| | |
|---|---|
| 1/2 | cup butter, softened |
| 2/3 | cup packed brown sugar |
| 2 | egg yolks |
| 1 | teaspoon vanilla extract |
| 1-1/2 | cups all-purpose flour |
| 1/2 | teaspoon baking powder |
| 1/2 | teaspoon salt |
| 1/4 | teaspoon baking soda |
| 3 | cups miniature marshmallows |

**TOPPING:**

| | |
|---|---|
| 2/3 | cup corn syrup |
| 1/4 | cup butter, softened |
| 1 | package (10 ounces) peanut butter chips |
| 2 | teaspoons vanilla extract |
| 2 | cups crisp rice cereal |
| 1 | cup salted peanuts |
| 1 | cup milk chocolate M&M's |

In a large mixing bowl, cream butter and brown sugar until light and fluffy. Beat in egg yolks and vanilla. Combine the flour, baking powder, salt and baking soda; gradually add to the creamed mixture until mixture resembles coarse crumbs (do not overmix).

Press into a greased 13-in. x 9-in. x 2-in. baking pan. Bake at 350° for 12-14 minutes or until golden brown. Immediately sprinkle with marshmallows; bake 2-3 minutes longer or until marshmallows are puffed. Cool on a wire rack.

For topping, in a large saucepan, combine the corn syrup, butter and peanut butter chips. Cook and stir over medium heat until chips are melted and mixture is smooth. Remove from the heat; stir in the vanilla, cereal, nuts and M&M's. Spread over crust. Cool before cutting. **Yield:** 2 dozen.

macadamia lemon bars

## Macadamia Lemon Bars

Edie DeSpain, Logan, Utah

"These bars melt in your mouth" and "They're out of this world" are compliments I receive frequently when people taste this treat. They are excellent for showers and other get-togethers.

| | |
|---|---|
| 1 | cup all-purpose flour |
| 1/4 | cup confectioners' sugar |
| 1/2 | cup butter, melted |
| 1/4 | cup chopped macadamia nuts |

**FILLING:**

| | |
|---|---|
| 1 | cup sugar |
| 2 | tablespoons all-purpose flour |
| 1/2 | teaspoon baking powder |
| 1/4 | teaspoon salt |
| 2 | eggs |
| 2 | tablespoons lemon juice |
| 2 | teaspoons grated lemon peel |
| 2 | tablespoons chopped macadamia nuts |

Confectioners' sugar

In a large bowl, combine the flour, confectioners' sugar and butter until crumbly; stir in nuts.

Press onto the bottom and 1/2 in. up the sides of a greased 8-in. square baking dish. Bake at 350° for 15-20 minutes or until lightly browned.

In a small mixing bowl, combine the sugar, flour, baking powder and salt. Beat in the eggs, lemon juice and lemon peel until light and fluffy.

Pour over hot crust. Sprinkle with nuts. Bake for 10-15 minutes or until lightly browned. Cool completely on a wire rack. Cut into bars. Sprinkle with the confectioners' sugar. **Yield:** 1 dozen.

## Toffee Squares

Judith Scholovich, Waukesha, Wisconsin

These easy, candy-like bars are very rich, so I cut them into smaller bars. Using German sweet chocolate gives them a delightfully different taste.

candy cereal treats

1 cup butter, softened
1 cup packed brown sugar
1 egg yolk
1 teaspoon vanilla extract
2 cups all-purpose flour
1/4 teaspoon salt
2 packages (4 ounces *each*) German sweet chocolate
1/2 cup chopped nuts

In a large mixing bowl, cream butter and brown sugar until light and fluffy. Add the egg yolk, vanilla, flour and salt; mix well. Spread into a greased 13-in. x 9-in. x 2-in. baking pan.

Bake at 350° for 20-25 minutes or until golden brown. In a heavy saucepan or microwave, melt chocolate; stir until smooth. Spread over hot bars. Immediately sprinkle with nuts. Cool on a wire rack. Cut into 1-1/4-in. squares. **Yield:** 4-1/2 dozen.

## Chocolate Peanut Butter Treats
Sue McLaughlin, Onawa, Iowa

For true chocolate lovers, you can eliminate the butterscotch chips if you like and use all chocolate chips. Either way, these no-bake snacks are simple and delicious.

1/4 cup butter, cubed
1 package (10 ounces) marshmallows
3/4 cup creamy peanut butter
5 cups crisp rice cereal
1 cup butterscotch chips
1 cup (6 ounces) semisweet chocolate chips

In a microwave, melt butter and marshmallows; stir until smooth. Remove from the heat; stir in peanut butter until smooth. Gradually add cereal; toss to coat. Spread and press into a greased 13-in. x 9-in. x 2-in. pan; set aside.

In a microwave, melt chips; stir to coat. Spread over cereal mixture. Cover and freeze for 15-20 minutes or until chocolate is set. **Yield:** 12-16 servings.

chocolate peanut butter treats

cinnamon brownies

## Cinnamon Brownies
Christopher Wolf, Belvidere, Illinois

No frosting is needed on top of these chewy, fudge-like brownies. This nice, basic bar has a burst of cinnamon in every bite.

3/4 cup butter, melted
1-2/3 cups sugar
2 tablespoons strong brewed coffee
2 eggs
2 teaspoons vanilla extract
1-1/3 cups all-purpose flour
3/4 cup baking cocoa
1 tablespoon ground cinnamon
1/2 teaspoon baking powder
1/4 teaspoon salt
1 cup chopped walnuts
Confectioners' sugar

In a large mixing bowl, beat the butter, sugar and coffee until smooth. Beat in eggs and vanilla. Combine the flour, cocoa, cinnamon, baking powder and salt; gradually add to the sugar mixture. Stir in walnuts.

Spread into a greased 13-in. x 9-in. x 2-in. baking pan. Bake at 350° for 18-22 minutes or until a toothpick inserted near the center comes out clean (do not overbake). Cool on a wire rack. Dust with confectioners' sugar. **Yield:** 2 dozen.

# Brownie Point

For easier cleanup, bake brownies in a foil-lined pan. Use the foil to lift them out once cooled.

chocolate chip cake bars

## Chocolate Chip Cake Bars

Tammy Haugen, Mayville, Wisconsin

Whenever I need a quick dessert for a bake sale or get-together, I rely on this specialty. I keep cake mixes on hand, so these chocolate chip-studded treats are a snap to stir up.

| | |
|---|---|
| 1 | package (18-1/4 ounces) yellow cake mix |
| 2 | eggs |
| 1/4 | cup packed brown sugar |
| 1/4 | cup butter, melted |
| 1/4 | cup water |
| 2 | cups (12 ounces) semisweet chocolate chips, *divided* |
| 1/2 | cup chopped pecans *or* walnuts |
| 1 | tablespoon shortening |

In a large mixing bowl, combine the first five ingredients. Beat on medium speed for 2 minutes. Stir in 1-1/2 cups of chocolate chips and nuts.

Spread in a greased 13-in. x 9-in. x 2-in. baking pan. Bake at 375° for 20-25 minutes or until lightly browned and a toothpick inserted near the center comes out clean. Cool on a wire rack.

Melt shortening with the remaining chocolate chips; drizzle over the top. Cut into bars. **Yield:** about 3-1/2 dozen.

## Peanut Butter-Honey Bars

Janet Hamacher, La Moille, Illinois

If you're in a hurry in the morning, just one of these bars with a glass of milk gets you started on the right foot. And if you have a hungry crew to feed, the recipe can be easily doubled.

| | |
|---|---|
| 1/2 | cup peanut butter |
| 2 | eggs, lightly beaten |
| 1/4 | cup honey |
| 2/3 | cup nonfat dry milk powder |
| 3 | cups fruit and fiber cereal (any flavor) |

In a large bowl, combine the peanut butter, eggs and honey until smooth. Stir in milk powder. Add cereal; toss to coat.

Spread in a greased 8-in. square baking pan. Bake at 325° for 20 minutes (mixture may look damp). Cool and cut into bars. Store in refrigerator. **Yield:** 6 servings.

## No-Bake Raisin Bars

Dawn Fagerstrom, Warren, Minnesota

Hearty snacks like these really fight hunger on the road. They come together in moments and are ideal for eating on the run.

| | |
|---|---|
| 3 | cups miniature marshmallows |
| 1/4 | cup butter, cubed |
| 5 | cups multi-grain puffed rice cereal |
| 1 | cup raisins |
| 1/2 | cup chopped walnuts |
| 1/4 | teaspoon ground cinnamon |

In a large saucepan, melt marshmallows and butter over low heat; stir until smooth. Stir in the cereal, raisins, walnuts and cinnamon; toss to coat. Pat into a greased 13 x 9 x 2-inch baking pan. Cool. Cut into bars. **Yield:** 2 dozen.

## Peanutty Caramel Bars

Charlene Bennett, Cedarville, Pennsylvania

Made in the microwave, these sweet and chewy bars can be stirred in a pinch. Loaded with caramel, chocolate, peanuts and peanut butter, they remind some folks of a popular candy bar.

peanutty caramel bars

classic lemon bars

Meanwhile, in another small mixing bowl, beat the eggs, sugar, lemon juice, flour and baking powder until frothy. Pour over warm crust.

Bake for 15-20 minutes longer or until lightly browned. Cool on a wire rack. Dust with confectioners' sugar. Cut into bars. **Yield:** 9 servings.

## Chewy Granola Bars

Alice McVey, Evansville, Indiana

This scrumptious treat is full of goodies like marshmallows, raisins, chocolate chips and sunflower kernels.

```
1       package (10-1/2 ounces) large marshmallows
2/3     cup chunky peanut butter
1/2     cup butter, cubed
1/4     cup corn syrup
2       teaspoons vanilla extract
4       cups quick-cooking oats
1       cup crisp rice cereal
1       cup (6 ounces) miniature semisweet chocolate
        chips
1/2     cup flaked coconut
1/2     cup sunflower kernels
1/2     cup chopped peanuts
1/2     cup raisins
2       tablespoons toasted wheat germ
2       tablespoons sesame seeds
```

In a large microwave-safe bowl, combine the marshmallows, peanut butter, butter, corn syrup and vanilla. Microwave, uncovered, at 70% power for 2-3 minutes, stirring often until blended. Stir in the remaining ingredients.

Spread into a greased 13-in. x 9-in. x 2-in. baking pan. Bake at 350° for 15-20 minutes or until set. Cool on a wire rack. Cut into bars. **Yield:** 2 dozen.

***Editor's Note:*** *Reduced-fat or generic brands of peanut butter are not recommended for this recipe.*

```
1       package (14 ounces) caramels
1/4     cup water
3/4     cup peanut butter, divided
4       cups Cheerios
1       cup salted peanuts
1       cup (6 ounces) semisweet chocolate chips or
        1 cup milk chocolate chips
1/2     cup butter, softened
```

In a large microwave-safe bowl, heat caramels, water and 1/2 cup peanut butter on high for 45 seconds; stir. Microwave 1 to 1-1/2 minutes longer or until melted. Add cereal and peanuts; toss to coat. Spread into a greased 13-in. x 9-in. x 2-in. pan; set aside.

In another microwave-safe bowl, heat chips, butter and remaining peanut butter on high for 20-50 seconds or until melted. Spread over cereal mixture. Refrigerate before cutting. **Yield:** about 3 dozen.

***Editor's Note:*** *This recipe was tested with a 1100-watt microwave. Reduced-fat or generic brands of peanut butter are not recommended for this recipe.*

## Classic Lemon Bars

Melissa Mosness, Loveland, Colorado

Looking for old-fashioned taste without a lot of effort? Give Classic Lemon Bars a try. You'll be amazed at how quickly the yummy snacks come together.

```
1/2     cup butter, softened
1/4     cup sugar
1       cup all-purpose flour
FILLING:
2       eggs
3/4     cup sugar
3       tablespoons lemon juice
2       tablespoons all-purpose flour
1/4     teaspoon baking powder
Confectioners' sugar
```

In a small mixing bowl, cream butter and sugar until light and fluffy; gradually add flour.

Press into an ungreased 8-in. square baking dish. Bake at 375° for 12 minutes. Cool slightly.

chewy granola bars

m&m oat bars

## M&M Oat Bars

Renee Schwebach, Dumont, Minnesota

These irresistible bars make for a simple way to sweeten any holiday.

       1/2   cup butter, softened
         1   cup packed brown sugar
         1   egg
         1   teaspoon vanilla extract
     1-1/4   cups all-purpose flour
       1/2   teaspoon baking soda
       1/2   teaspoon salt
         2   cups quick-cooking oats
         1   package (14 ounces) caramels
         3   tablespoons water
         1   cup (6 ounces) miniature semisweet chocolate chips
         1   cup chopped walnuts
         1   cup plain M&M's
         3   ounces white confectionery coating

In a large mixing bowl, cream butter and brown sugar until light and fluffy. Beat in egg and vanilla. Combine the flour, baking soda and salt; add to the creamed mixture. Stir in oats.

Press into a greased 15-in. x 10-in. x 1-in. baking pan. Bake at 350° for 10-15 minutes or until golden brown. Cool on a wire rack.

In a microwave-safe bowl, melt caramels and water; stir until smooth. Spread over crust. Sprinkle with the chips, nuts and M&M's. Gently press into the caramel mixture. Melt confectionery coating; drizzle over the top. Let stand for 5 minutes or until coating is set. Cut into bars. **Yield:** 6 dozen.

## Nutty Brownies

Neva Mathes, Pella, Iowa

I often whip up these tasty brownies when unexpected guests stop by. They always receive favorable comments, and they also make a fast dessert to take along to a picnic.

       1/2   cup butter, melted
         1   cup sugar
         2   eggs
         1   teaspoon vanilla extract
       3/4   cup all-purpose flour
       1/3   cup baking cocoa
       1/2   teaspoon salt
         1   cup chopped nuts
Confectioners' sugar, optional

In a large mixing bowl, cream butter and sugar until light and fluffy. Beat in eggs and vanilla. Combine the flour, cocoa and salt; gradually add to butter mixture just until combined. Stir in nuts. Spread into a greased microwave-safe 8-in. square dish.

Microwave, uncovered, on high for 3-1/2 to 4 minutes or until top appears dry and springs back when lightly touched. Dust with confectioners' sugar if desired. **Yield:** about 1-1/2 dozen.

*Editor's Note: This recipe was tested in a 1,100-watt microwave.*

## Peanut Cookie Bars

Gaylene Anderson, Sandy, Utah

Looking for a quick snack? Try my peanut-flavored bars. You'll enjoy each nutty bite, and you won't waste a lot of time in the kitchen putting them together.

        12   cups cornflakes, crushed
         1   jar (16 ounces) dry roasted peanuts
     1-1/2   cups corn syrup
         1   cup sugar
         1   cup packed brown sugar
         1   cup peanut butter

In a large bowl, combine cornflakes and peanuts. In a large saucepan, combine corn syrup and sugars; bring to a boil. Boil for 1 minute. Remove from the heat; stir in peanut butter.

Pour over cornflake mixture; toss to coat. Press into a greased 15-in. x 10-in. x 1-in. baking pan. Cool slightly; cut into bars. **Yield:** 2 dozen.

peanut cookie bars

## Quick Brownies

Mrs. Ed Fitch, Clifton, Arizona

A chocolate cake mix makes my brownies a cinch to stir up, but peanut butter chips give them an extra flavor boost.

- 1 package (18-1/4 ounces) chocolate cake mix
- 1/2 cup butter, melted
- 1/2 cup vegetable oil
- 2 eggs
- 1 cup peanut butter chips

In a large mixing bowl, beat the first four ingredients until blended. Stir in chips.

Pour into a greased 11-in. x 7-in. x 2-in. baking pan. Bake at 350° for 35-40 minutes or until a toothpick inserted near the center comes out clean. Cool on a wire rack. **Yield:** 18 servings.

## Peanut Butter Brownie Cups

Karen Presbrey, Pascoag, Rhode Island

Two items are all you need to whip up these fudgy brownie cups with peanut butter centers. You're gang will request them time and again!

- 1 package (21-1/2 ounces) fudge brownie mix
- 15 to 18 miniature peanut butter cups

Mix brownie batter according to package directions. Fill paper-lined or foil-lined muffin cups two-thirds full.

Remove wrappers from peanut butter cups; set one in each muffin cup and press down until batter meets the top edge of the candy. Bake at 350° for 20-25 minutes. Cool in pan for 5 minutes before removing to a wire rack to cool completely. **Yield:** about 1-1/2 dozen.

peanut butter brownie cups

fun marshmallow bars

## Fun Marshmallow Bars

Debbie Brunssen, Randolph, Nebraska

For colorful, kid-tested treats that go fast at bake sales, give my recipe a try. Cake mix really cuts the prep time.

- 1 package (18-1/4 ounces) devil's food cake mix
- 1/4 cup butter, melted
- 1/4 cup water
- 1 egg
- 3 cups miniature marshmallows
- 1 cup milk chocolate M&M's
- 1/2 cup chopped peanuts

In a large mixing bowl, combine the dry cake mix, butter, water and egg. Press into a greased 13-in. x 9-in. x 2-in. baking pan. Bake at 375° for 20-22 minutes or until a toothpick inserted near the center comes out clean.

Sprinkle with marshmallows, M&M's and peanuts. Bake 2-3 minutes longer or until the marshmallows begin to melt. Cool on a wire rack. Cut into bars. **Yield:** 3-1/2 dozen.

# Brownie Point

When cutting brownies, try not to use a sawing motion. Cutting downward with a serrated knife usually results in uniform, eye-appealing goodies. When slicing frosted snacks, be sure to wipe the knife clean between cuts.

peppermint oat bars

## Peppermint Oat Bars

Connie Major Williams, Dexter, Michigan

Peppermint and chocolate chips are a terrific combination in my oat bars. The first time my brother-in-law tasted them, he said, "Mmmm...can you buy these someplace?"

       1 cup all-purpose flour
     1/2 cup quick-cooking oats
     1/3 cup sugar
     1/3 cup butter, melted
     1/3 cup chopped walnuts
       4 ounces cream cheese, softened
       1 egg
     1/2 teaspoon vanilla extract
     1/3 cup semisweet chocolate chips
     1/3 to 1/2 cup crushed peppermint candies

In a large bowl, combine the flour, oats, sugar and butter. Stir in nuts (mixture will be crumbly). Set aside 3/4 cup for topping.

Press the remaining mixture into a greased 9-in. square baking pan. Bake at 350° for 10-12 minutes or until lightly browned. Cool on a wire rack.

In a large mixing bowl, beat cream cheese until fluffy. Beat in egg and vanilla. Stir in chocolate chips and peppermint candies.

Pour over crust; sprinkle with reserved crumb mixture. Bake at 350° for 20-22 minutes or until lightly browned. Cool on a wire rack. Cut into bars. Store in refrigerator. **Yield:** about 1-1/2 dozen.

## Saucepan Brownies

Dorelene Doddridge, Kirk, Colorado

Preparing a brownie batter in a saucepan with biscuit mix may sound odd, but it sure cuts down on prep time. You won't believe the delicious results.

       1 cup (6 ounces) semisweet chocolate chips
     1/4 cup butter, cubed
       2 cups biscuit/baking mix
       1 can (14 ounces) sweetened condensed milk
       1 egg, lightly beaten
       1 cup chopped walnuts

In a large saucepan, melt chocolate chips and butter over low heat. Stir until well blended; remove from the heat. Stir in the biscuit mix, milk and egg until smooth. Add nuts.

Pour into greased 13-in. x 9-in. x 2-in. baking pan. Bake at 350° for 25 minutes. **Yield:** 2-1/2 dozen.

## Rich Cheesecake Bars

Tammy Helle, St. Louis, Missouri

I take turns with some of the ladies at church to provide coffee-time snacks for adult Bible class and Sunday school. These gooey bars, a traditional St. Louis dessert, are a favorite.

       1 package (9 ounces) yellow cake mix
       3 tablespoons butter, softened
       1 egg
TOPPING:
       1 package (3 ounces) cream cheese, softened
       2 cups confectioners' sugar
       1 egg

In a large mixing bowl, combine the dry cake mix, butter and egg. Spread into a greased 9-in. square baking pan.

In a small mixing bowl, combine the cream cheese, confectioners' sugar and egg; spread evenly over batter.

Bake at 350° for 30-35 minutes or until a toothpick inserted near the center comes out clean. Cool on a wire rack. Store in the refrigerator. **Yield:** 2 dozen.

rich cheesecake bars

spice bars

## Spice Bars

Brooke Pike, Durham, North Carolina

With their sensational aroma, these spiced treats bring everyone to the kitchen in a hurry! Try a bar with a cup of coffee on a fall day.

- 6 tablespoons buttermilk
- 1/3 cup packed brown sugar
- 1/4 cup molasses
- 3 tablespoons butter, melted
- 1 egg
- 1 teaspoon vanilla extract
- 1-1/4 cups all-purpose flour
- 3/4 teaspoon ground cinnamon, *divided*
- 1-1/4 teaspoons Chinese five-spice powder
- 1/2 teaspoon baking powder
- 1/4 teaspoon baking soda
- 1/4 teaspoon salt
- 1/3 cup raisins
- 1 tablespoon confectioners' sugar

In a large mixing bowl, beat the buttermilk, brown sugar, molasses, butter, egg and vanilla until smooth. Combine the flour, 1/2 teaspoon cinnamon, five-spice powder, baking powder, baking soda and salt; gradually add to buttermilk mixture and beat until smooth. Stir in raisins.

Pour into a 9-in. square baking pan coated with nonstick cooking spray. Bake at 350° for 18-20 minutes or until a toothpick inserted near the center comes out clean. Cool on a wire rack. Combine confectioners' sugar and remaining cinnamon; sprinkle over bars. **Yield:** 1 dozen.

## Double Chocolate Brownies

Sue Gronholz, Columbus, Wisconsin

These rich, fudgy brownies can't be beat for a scrumptious dessert when you're racing against the clock.

- 1/2 cup butter, cubed
- 2 squares (1 ounce *each*) unsweetened chocolate
- 2 eggs
- 3/4 cup sugar
- 1/2 cup all-purpose flour

- 1 teaspoon baking powder
- 1 teaspoon vanilla extract
- 1/2 cup semisweet chocolate chips
Confectioners' sugar

In a microwave, melt butter and chocolate; stir until smooth. Cool slightly. In a large mixing bowl, beat eggs for 2 minutes. Gradually add sugar, beating until thick and pale yellow. Combine flour and baking powder; add to egg mixture. Stir in melted chocolate, vanilla and chips.

Pour into a greased 8-in. square microwave-safe baking dish. Cook on high for 3-1/2 to 4 minutes. Remove to a wire rack; cool for 10 minutes. Dust with confectioners' sugar. **Yield:** 1 dozen.

## Sunflower Popcorn Bars

Karen Ann Bland, Gove, Kansas

Kansas is called the Sunflower State because of the wild sunflowers that grow abundantly. My popcorn balls are a great way to use those tasty sunflower kernels.

- 1 cup sugar
- 1/2 cup light corn syrup
- 1/2 cup honey
- 1/2 cup peanut butter
- 1/4 cup butter, softened
- 1 teaspoon vanilla extract
- 1 cup salted sunflower kernels
- 4 quarts popped popcorn

In a large saucepan over medium heat, bring the sugar, corn syrup and honey to a boil, stirring often. Boil for 2 minutes. Remove from the heat; stir in the peanut butter, butter and vanilla until smooth. Add sunflower kernels.

Place popcorn in a large bowl. Add syrup and stir to coat. Press into two greased 13-in. x 9-in. x 2-in. baking pans. Cut into bars. Store in an airtight container. **Yield:** 4 dozen.

***Editor's Note:*** *Reduced-fat or generic brands of peanut butter are not recommended for this recipe.*

sunflower popcorn bars

## Cranberry Popcorn Bars

Steve Dold, Monon, Indiana

Here's a fun change of pace. Popped popcorn, dried cranberries and walnuts steal the show in these bars.

- 6 cups popped popcorn
- 3 cups miniature marshmallows
- 1 tablespoon butter
- 1 cup dried cranberries, chopped
- 1 cup chopped walnuts
- 2 tablespoons grated orange peel
- 1/4 teaspoon salt

Place popcorn in a large bowl; set aside. In a large heavy saucepan, cook and stir marshmallows and butter over low heat until smooth. Stir in the cranberries, walnuts, orange peel and salt.

Pour over popcorn and toss to coat. Press into a greased 11-in. x 7-in. x 2-in. baking pan. Cool. Cut into bars with a serrated knife. **Yield:** 1 dozen.

## Diamond Bars

Lois Lipker, Ormond Beach, Florida

You'll need just seven basic ingredients to stir up a batch of these delicious snacks. Cutting them into diamonds makes for an interesting presentation.

- 1 cup butter, softened
- 1 cup packed brown sugar
- 2 egg yolks
- 2 cups all-purpose flour
- 2 cups (12 ounces) semisweet chocolate chips
- 1 cup chopped walnuts
- 1 cup flaked coconut

cranberry popcorn bars

In a large mixing bowl, cream the butter and brown sugar until light and fluffy. Beat in egg yolks. Gradually add flour until blended.

Spread into a greased 15-in. x 10-in. x 1-in. baking pan. Bake at 325° for 20-25 minutes or until golden brown.

Sprinkle with chocolate chips. Bake 1 minute longer or until chips are melted. Spread chocolate over crust. Sprinkle with walnuts and coconut. Cool on a wire rack. Cut into diamond shapes. **Yield:** 5 dozen.

## Fast Fudgy Brownies

Mary Sprick, New Haven, Missouri

For from-scratch brownies that don't tax your kitchen time, consider my time-savvy treat. Loaded with chocolate and cherry flavor, they're popular in my house.

- 1 cup vegetable oil
- 4 eggs
- 1 teaspoon vanilla extract
- 2 cups sugar
- 1-1/3 cups all-purpose flour
- 1/2 cup baking cocoa
- 1 teaspoon salt
- 1 cup (6 ounces) semisweet chocolate chips
- 1/2 cup chopped maraschino cherries *or* nuts, optional

In a large mixing bowl, beat the oil, eggs and vanilla on medium speed for 1 minute. Combine the sugar, flour, cocoa and salt; gradually add to egg mixture just until blended. Stir in chocolate chips and cherries or nuts.

Pour into a greased 13-in. x 9-in. x 2-in. baking pan. Bake at 350° for 30-35 minutes or until a toothpick inserted near the center comes out with moist crumbs (do not overbake). Cool on a wire rack. Cut into bars. **Yield:** 2 dozen.

diamond bars

layered brownie cookies

## Layered Brownie Cookies
Amy Corey, Monticello, Maine

Graham crackers are sandwiched between a brownie base and chocolate chip cookie top in these treats. My mother made them for us, and now I make them for my children.

    3/4   cup butter, softened
      1   cup sugar
      2   eggs
    1/3   cup milk
      1   teaspoon vanilla extract
  1-3/4   cups all-purpose flour
      1   teaspoon salt
      1   teaspoon baking soda
      1   square (1 ounce) semisweet chocolate,
          melted
    3/4   cup chopped walnuts
      9   whole graham crackers
    3/4   cup semisweet chocolate chips

In a large mixing bowl, cream butter and sugar until light and fluffy. Add eggs, one at a time, beating well after each addition. Combine milk and vanilla. Combine flour, salt and baking soda; add to the creamed mixture alternately with milk mixture.

Remove a third of the batter to another bowl; stir in melted chocolate. Fold in walnuts. Spread into a greased 13-in. x 9-in. x 2-in. baking pan. Arrange graham crackers over top.

Add chocolate chips to remaining batter. Drop by spoonfuls over graham crackers and spread evenly. Bake at 375° for 20-25 minutes or until top springs back when lightly touched. Cool on a wire rack before cutting. **Yield:** 2 dozen.

## Banana Crunch Bars
Ruth Anderson, Clarion, Iowa

The distinctive taste of banana tops these easy-to-make, no-bake cereal bars. The fruity flavor is a refreshing change from most other brownies.

      1   cup sugar
      1   cup corn syrup
  1-1/2   cups crunchy peanut butter
      5   cups Banana Nut Crunch cereal
      1   package (11-1/2 ounces) milk chocolate chips

In a microwave-safe bowl, combine sugar and corn syrup. Microwave, uncovered, on high for 2-3 minutes or until sugar is dissolved. Stir in peanut butter. Add cereal; stir to coat.

Press into a greased 13-in. x 9-in. x 2-in. pan. In a microwave-safe bowl, melt chocolate chips; stir until smooth. Spread over bars. Cool before cutting. **Yield:** about 4-1/2 dozen.

*Editor's Note:* This recipe was tested in a 1,100-watt microwave.

## Double Chip Bars
Victoria Lowe, Lititz, Pennsylvania

Our children love the combination of peanut butter and chocolate in these dessert bars. The snacks go together so quickly that I can make them on a moment's notice or even on my busiest days. They're perfect for school treats and charity bake sales.

    1/2   cup butter, melted
  1-1/2   cups graham cracker crumbs
      1   can (14 ounces) sweetened condensed milk
      2   cups (12 ounces) semisweet chocolate chips
      1   cup peanut butter chips

Place butter in a 13-in. x 9-in. x 2-in. baking pan. Sprinkle the cracker crumbs evenly over butter. Pour milk evenly over crumbs. Sprinkle with chips; press down firmly.

Bake at 350° for 25-30 minutes or until golden brown. Cool on a wire rack before cutting. **Yield:** 3 dozen.

double chip bars

# Chapter 7

p. 102

p. 96

p. 100

p. 105

p. 106

# Brownie Desserts

Everyone loves brownies, but when you need something extra special, turn to these lavish showstoppers. The dressed-up brownies make for easy yet impressive dinner finales.

triple layer brownie cake

## Triple Layer Brownie Cake

Barbara Dean, Littleton, Colorado

A little of this rich brownie cake goes a long way, so you'll have plenty to share with grateful family members and friends. It's a sure way to satisfy chocolate lovers.

- 1-1/2 cups butter
- 6 squares (1 ounce *each*) unsweetened chocolate
- 3 cups sugar
- 5 eggs
- 1-1/2 teaspoons vanilla extract
- 1-1/2 cups all-purpose flour
- 3/4 teaspoon salt

FROSTING:
- 2 packages (8 ounces *each*) semisweet chocolate
- 3 cups heavy whipping cream
- 1/2 cup sugar, optional
- 2 milk chocolate candy bars (1.55 ounces *each*), shaved

In a microwave or double boiler, melt butter and chocolate. Stir in sugar. Add eggs, one at a time, beating well after each addition. Stir in vanilla, flour and salt; mix well. Pour into three greased and floured 9-in. round cake pans. Bake at 350° for 23-25 minutes or until a toothpick inserted near the center comes out clean. Cool for 10 minutes; remove from pan to a wire rack to cool completely.

For frosting, melt chocolate in a heavy saucepan over medium heat. Gradually stir in cream and sugar if desired, until well blended. Heat to a gentle boil; boil and stir for 1 minute. Remove from the heat; transfer to a mixing bowl. Refrigerate for 2-3 hours or until mixture reaches a pudding-like consistency, stirring a few times. Beat until soft peaks form. Immediately spread between layers and over top and sides of cake. Sprinkle with shaved chocolate. Store in the refrigerator. **Yield:** 16-20 servings.

## Layered Brownie Dessert

Muriel Ledeboer, Oostburg, Wisconsin

A tasty brownie is the base for cream cheese and chocolate pudding layers in this make-ahead dessert.

- 1 cup butter, softened
- 2 cups sugar
- 2 eggs
- 1 teaspoon vanilla extract
- 2 cups all-purpose flour
- 1/2 cup baking cocoa
- 1/2 teaspoon salt
- 1/2 teaspoon baking powder
- 1 cup chopped walnuts

FILLING:
- 2 packages (one 8 ounces, one 3 ounces) cream cheese, softened
- 2 cups confectioners' sugar
- 2 cups whipped topping

TOPPING:
- 2 cups cold milk
- 1 package (3.9 ounces) instant chocolate pudding mix

Whipped topping and chopped walnuts

In a large mixing bowl, cream butter and sugar. Add eggs, one at a time, beating well after each addition. Add vanilla. Combine the flour, cocoa, salt and baking powder; add to creamed mixture just until moistened. Stir in nuts.

Transfer to a greased 13-in. x 9-in. x 2-in. baking pan. Bake at 350° for 20-25 minutes or until a toothpick inserted near the center comes out clean. Cool completely on a wire rack.

In a small mixing bowl, beat cream cheese and con-

layered brownie dessert

strawberry brownie bombe

ie may crack). Spread preserves over brownie layer. Freeze for 15 minutes. Fill brownie-lined bowl with ice cream; smooth top. Cover and freeze for 3 hours or until ice cream is firm.

Place remaining brownie layer on a serving plate. Remove bowl from freezer; uncover. Invert onto brownie layer; remove bowl and foil. Return dessert to freezer.

In a large mixing bowl, beat cream and food coloring until soft peaks form. Add sugar and beat until stiff peaks form; set aside 1-1/2 cups. Spread remaining whipped cream over top and sides of bombe.

Cut a small hole in the corner of a pastry or plastic bag and insert star tip. Fill with reserved whipped cream; pipe border at base of bombe. Holding the bag straight up and down, form stars on top. Garnish with strawberries and mint if desired. **Yield:** 16 servings.

## Mini Brownie Treats

Pam Kokes, North Loup, Nebraska

I like to take these two-ingredient goodies to potlucks and family gatherings. They come together in no time at all, and they always disappear in a flash!

> 1    **package fudge brownie mix (13-inch x 9-inch pan size)**
> 48   **striped chocolate kisses**

Prepare brownie mix according to package directions for fudge-like brownies. Fill paper-lined miniature muffin cups two-thirds full.

Bake at 350° for 18-21 minutes or until a toothpick comes out clean. Immediately top each with a chocolate kiss. Cool for 10 minutes before removing from pans to wire racks to cool completely. **Yield:** 4 dozen.

fectioners' sugar until smooth. Fold in whipped topping; spread over brownies. In a bowl, whisk milk and pudding mix for 2 minutes. Let stand for 2 minutes or until soft-set. Spread over filling. Refrigerate for 1 hour or until serving.

Cut into squares; garnish with whipped topping and nuts. **Yield:** 12-15 servings.

## Strawberry Brownie Bombe

Joanne Watts, Kitchener, Ontario

A friend and I dreamed up this recipe. We use it to entertain and for special family dinners. For an extra touch, you can dip the strawberries in chocolate.

> 1    **package fudge brownie mix (13-inch x 9-inch pan size)**
> 1/2   **cup chopped walnuts**
> 1/2   **cup strawberry preserves**
> 1    **quart strawberry ice cream, softened**
> 2    **cups heavy whipping cream**
> 3    **drops red food coloring, optional**
> 1/4   **cup confectioners' sugar**
> **Fresh strawberries and mint, optional**

Prepare brownie mix according to package directions for cake-like brownies. Stir in walnuts. Pour the batter into two greased and waxed paper-lined 8-in. round baking pans. Bake at 350° for 30 minutes or until a toothpick inserted near the center comes out clean. Cool completely in pans.

Line a 1-1/2-qt. metal bowl with foil. Cut and fit one brownie layer to evenly line the inside of a bowl (brown-

mini brownie treats

# Extra Brownies Make Incredibly Easy Edibles

## You'll beat the kitchen clock by featuring yesterday's brownies in tonight's after-dinner sensation!

Today, family bakers have lots of no-fuss tricks to help them shave minutes from prep work. One idea is to make extra food to ensure there's plenty of leftovers on hand.

The next step is to take those "planned overs," and turn them into completely different items, each loaded with flavor as well as time-easing convenience.

For instance, you can easily surprise your gang with a terrific dessert by taking advantage of the extra brownies you prepared the night before. Simply crumble the leftover brownies into a large bowl and stir in some softened ice cream.

Flavors such as mint, coffee and strawberry make tasty choices, but feel free to use vanilla or whatever ice cream variety you have on hand. Cover the bowl and set it back in the freezer for a bit. Even those who say they don't like leftovers are sure to enjoy mouth-watering scoops of this frosty treat.

If you just don't have time to get your creative juices flowing, consider baking up a batch of No-Fuss Fudgy Brownies using the recipe at top right.

The homemade snacks are great on their own, but the extras are fantastic when worked into the filling of Brownie Cheesecake. Or, try layering them into Mocha Mousse Brownie Trifle. The cheesecake and trifle recipes appear at right and both call for prepared brownies.

Turn to this trio of brownie desserts when your schedule is swarming. After all, with sweet sensations this good, no one will suspect how easily they all came together.

## No-Fuss Fudgy Brownies
June Formanek, Belle Plaine, Iowa

I've made these moist brownies many times and they're always a hit with my family. Best of all, the recipe makes a lot so there are always leftovers to enjoy.

- 4 squares (1 ounce *each*) unsweetened chocolate
- 1 cup butter, cubed
- 4 eggs
- 2 cups sugar
- 1 teaspoon vanilla extract
- 1 cup all-purpose flour
- 1 cup (6 ounces) semisweet chocolate chips
- 1 cup chopped pecans, optional

Confectioners' sugar

In a microwave, melt chocolate and butter; stir until smooth. In a large mixing bowl, beat eggs, sugar and vanilla for 1-2 minutes or until light and lemon-colored. Beat in the chocolate mixture. Add flour; beat just until combined. Fold in chocolate chips and pecans if desired.

Transfer to a greased 13-in. x 9-in. x 2-in. baking pan. Bake at 350° for 25-30 minutes or until a toothpick inserted near the center comes out with moist crumbs. Cool on a wire rack. Dust with confectioners' sugar. **Yield:** 16-20 servings.

## Brownie Cheesecake
Dorothy Olivares, El Paso, Texas

I don't remember where I got this recipe, but it's so good! Before baking the smooth and creamy chocolate cheesecake, I crumble up prepared brownies and stir them into the batter for a delectable touch.

- 1-1/2 cups crushed vanilla wafers (about 45 cookies)
- 6 tablespoons confectioners' sugar
- 6 tablespoons baking cocoa
- 6 tablespoons butter, melted

FILLING:
- 3 packages (8 ounces *each*) cream cheese, softened
- 1/4 cup butter, melted
- 1 can (14 ounces) sweetened condensed milk
- 3 teaspoons vanilla extract
- 1/2 cup baking cocoa
- 4 eggs, lightly beaten
- 1-1/2 cups crumbled brownies

Whipped topping and pecan halves, optional

In a small bowl, combine the wafer crumbs, confectioners' sugar and cocoa; stir in the butter. Press onto the bottom of a greased 9-in. springform pan; set aside.

In a large mixing bowl, beat the cream cheese and butter until smooth. Add the milk and vanilla; mix well. Add the cocoa; mix well. Add eggs; beat on low just until combined. Fold in brownies. Spoon into crust. Place pan on a baking sheet.

Bake at 350° for 50-55 minutes or until center is almost set. Cool on a wire rack for 10 minutes. Carefully

run a knife around the edge of pan to loosen. Cool 1 hour longer. Refrigerate overnight.

Remove sides of pan. Garnish with whipped topping and pecans if desired. Refrigerate leftovers. **Yield:** 10-12 servings.

## Mocha Mousse Brownie Trifle

Taste of Home Test Kitchen

Our home economists used extra brownies to create this tempting, time-saving trifle. It's a snap to assemble with a packaged mousse mix and whipped topping.

    5    cups prepared brownies, cubed
    1    package (2.8 ounces) mocha mousse mix
    1    carton (12 ounces) frozen whipped topping, thawed
1/4    cup English toffee bits *or* almond brickle chips
**Grated chocolate**

Place half of the cubed brownies in a 2-qt. serving bowl. Prepare mousse mix according to package directions. Spread half over the brownies. Top with half of the whipped topping; sprinkle with toffee bits. Repeat layers of brownies, mousse and whipped topping. Sprinkle with grated chocolate. Refrigerate until serving. **Yield:** 10-12 servings.

## Brownie Point

Brownies and ice cream are a classic combo that makes for a tasty, in-a-flash dessert. A simple fix is to top individual servings with a scoop of vanilla and some hot fudge. If you want to try something a bit more decadent, however, press crumbled brownies into a pie pan. Spoon softened ice cream over this crust and top it all with a thin layer of your favorite jam. Next, drizzle chocolate or butterscotch ice cream toppings over the jam. Cover and freeze until it's time for dessert. Serve wedges with whipped cream.

giant ice cream sandwich

## Giant Ice Cream Sandwich

Charlene Turnbull, Wainwright, Alberta

I was an inexperienced baker when I married. A good friend, who was a cooking inspiration to me, shared many of her recipes, including this scrumptious dessert. It's handy to pull out of the freezer for unexpected guests.

    2   packages fudge brownie mix (8-inch square pan size)
    1   cup (6 ounces) semisweet chocolate chips
    4   cups vanilla ice cream, softened
1/2   cup English toffee bits *or* almond brickle chips
**CHOCOLATE SAUCE:**
1/3   cup evaporated milk
1/4   cup butter
1/3   cup semisweet chocolate chips
    2   cups confectioners' sugar
1/2   teaspoon vanilla extract

Prepare the brownie mixes according to package directions, adding the chocolate chips to batter. Pour into two greased 9-in. springform pans or two 9-in. round cake pans.

Bake at 350° for 25-30 minutes or until a toothpick inserted near the center comes out clean. Cool for 10 minutes before removing from pans to wire racks to cool completely. Freeze for 2 hours or until easy to handle.

Spoon ice cream on top of one brownie layer; top with toffee bits and second brownie layer. Wrap in plastic wrap; freeze until set. May be frozen for up to 2 months. Remove from the freezer 10-15 minutes before serving.

For chocolate sauce, in a small saucepan, combine the milk, butter and chocolate chips. Cook until chips are melted; stir until smooth. Stir in confectioners' sugar and vanilla. Cut the ice cream sandwich into wedges; serve with chocolate sauce. **Yield:** 10-12 servings.

## Cheesecake Brownies

James Harris, Columbus, Georgia

German chocolate cake mix and chopped nuts make a delicious change-of-pace crust for these brownies. Featuring a terrific cheesecake topping, the dessert is tough to beat.

    1   package (18-1/4 ounces) German chocolate cake mix
    1   egg, lightly beaten
1/2   cup butter, melted
    1   cup chopped nuts
**TOPPING:**
    1   package (8 ounces) cream cheese, softened
    1   cup sugar
    2   eggs, lightly beaten
    1   teaspoon vanilla extract

In a large mixing bowl, beat the cake mix, egg, butter and nuts until well blended. Press into a greased 13-in. x 9-in. x 2-in. baking pan; set aside.

In small mixing bowl, beat the cream cheese, sugar, eggs and vanilla until smooth. Carefully spread over the batter.

Bake at 350° for 30 to 35 minutes or until golden brown. Cool on a wire rack. Store in the refrigerator. **Yield:** 2 dozen.

## Brownie Caramel Parfaits

Chris Schnittka, Charlottesville, Virginia

It's easy to transform brownies, ice cream and caramel topping into a tempting treat. Layers of toasted coconut and chopped pecans add crunch and make this dessert seem fancy, but it couldn't be any simpler to assemble.

brownie caramel parfaits

mint brownie pie

1/2 cup chopped pecans
1/2 cup flaked coconut
1 package brownie mix (8-inch square pan size)
1 pint vanilla ice cream
1 jar (12-1/4 ounces) caramel ice cream topping

Place pecans and coconut in an ungreased baking pan. Bake at 350° for 10-12 minutes or until toasted, stirring frequently.

Meanwhile, prepare brownies according to package directions. Cool on a wire rack; cut into small squares.

When ready to serve, in six parfait or dessert glasses, layer the brownies, ice cream, caramel topping and pecan mixture; repeat layers one or two times. **Yield:** 6 servings.

## Mint Brownie Pie

Karen Hayes, Conneaut Lake, Pennsylvania

*When I served this pie to my family on St. Patrick's Day, it was an instant success. They loved the creamy, peppermint filling made pretty with a little green food coloring.*

6 tablespoons butter
2 squares (1 ounce *each*) unsweetened chocolate
1 cup sugar
2 eggs, lightly beaten
1/2 teaspoon vanilla extract
1/2 cup all-purpose flour
FILLING:
1 package (8 ounces) cream cheese, softened
3/4 cup sugar
1/2 teaspoon peppermint extract
Green food coloring, optional
1 carton (8 ounces) frozen whipped topping, thawed
1/4 cup semisweet chocolate chips, melted
Additional whipped topping and chocolate chips, optional

In a large saucepan, melt butter and chocolate. Stir in sugar until smooth. Add eggs and vanilla. Stir in flour until well blended.

Pour into a greased 9-in. springform pan. Bake at 350° for 18-20 minutes or until a toothpick inserted near the center comes out clean. Cool on a wire rack.

In a large mixing bowl, beat cream cheese and sugar until smooth. Beat in extract and food coloring if desired. Fold in whipped topping. Spread evenly over brownie layer. Cover and refrigerate for at least 1 hour.

Remove sides of pan just before serving. Melt chocolate chips; drizzle over the top. Garnish with whipped topping and additional chocolate chips if desired. **Yield:** 8 servings.

## Cupcake Brownies

Nila Towler, Baird, Texas

*These no-mess brownies travel very well. The nuts make the fudgy cupcakes extra special.*

1 cup butter, cubed
4 squares (1 ounce *each*) semisweet chocolate
4 eggs
1-3/4 cups sugar
1 teaspoon vanilla extract
1 cup all-purpose flour
1-1/2 cups chopped pecans

In a microwave, melt butter and chocolate; stir until smooth. Cool for 10 minutes.

In a large mixing bowl, beat eggs and sugar until blended. Beat in vanilla and chocolate mixture; gradually stir in flour and nuts.

Fill greased or paper-lined muffin cups two-thirds full. Bake at 350° for 18-20 minutes or until brownies test done with a toothpick. Cool. **Yield:** about 1-1/2 dozen.

cupcake brownies

## Brownie Pie a la Mode

Beverly Thornton, Cortlandt Manor, New York

This is an easy brownie recipe when you need something good, fancy and chocolaty without making a large amount.

  - 1/2   cup sugar
  - 2   tablespoons butter
  - 2   tablespoons water
  - 1-1/2   cups semisweet chocolate chips
  - 2   eggs
  - 1   teaspoon vanilla extract
  - 2/3   cup all-purpose flour
  - 1/4   teaspoon baking soda
  - 1/4   teaspoon salt
  - 3/4   cup chopped walnuts

**FUDGE SAUCE:**
  - 1   cup (6 ounces) semisweet chocolate chips
  - 1/2   cup evaporated milk
  - 1/4   cup sugar
  - 1   tablespoon butter

Vanilla ice cream

In a small saucepan, bring the sugar, butter and water to a boil over medium heat. Remove from the heat; stir in chocolate chips until melted. Set aside to cool.

In a large mixing bowl, beat eggs and vanilla. Add chocolate mixture; mix well. Combine the flour, baking soda and salt; add to the chocolate mixture. Stir in the walnuts.

Pour into a greased 9-in. pie plate. Bake at 350° for 28-30 minutes or until a toothpick inserted near the center comes out clean. Cool on a wire rack.

For fudge sauce, heat chocolate chips, milk, sugar and butter in a small heavy saucepan or microwave until chocolate and butter are melted; stir until smooth. Drizzle some over pie. Cut into wedges; serve with ice cream and additional fudge sauce. **Yield:** 6-8 servings.

brownie pie a la mode

banana split brownie pie

## Banana Split Brownie Pie

Tanna Walker, Salina, Kansas

I often use Neapolitan in place of the three different ice cream flavors to make this luscious dessert. You can even bake the brownie crust days ahead, top it with the ice cream and freeze until you need it. Feel free to add whatever toppings your family enjoys.

  - 4   ounces German sweet chocolate, chopped
  - 1/2   cup butter, cubed
  - 3   eggs
  - 1   cup sugar
  - 1/2   teaspoon vanilla extract
  - 1/2   cup all-purpose flour
  - 1-1/3   cups vanilla ice cream
  - 1-2/3   cups chocolate ice cream
  - 1-2/3   cups strawberry ice cream
  - 2   medium firm bananas, sliced
  - 1   cup fresh strawberries, sliced
  - 1/2   to 3/4 cup hot fudge ice cream topping, warmed
  - 1/2   to 3/4 cup strawberry ice cream topping
  - 1/4   to 1/2 cup toffee bits *or* almond brickle chips

Whipping cream and sliced almonds

In a microwave, melt chocolate and butter; stir until smooth. Cool. In a small mixing bowl, beat the eggs, sugar, vanilla and cooled chocolate mixture. Add flour; mix well. Spread into a greased 9-in. springform pan.

Bake at 350° for 30-35 minutes or until a toothpick inserted near the center comes out clean. Cool on a wire rack. Cover and freeze until firm.

Using 1/3 cup for each scoop, place four scoops of vanilla ice cream, five scoops of chocolate ice cream and five scoops of strawberry ice cream on a waxed paper-lined baking sheet. Freeze until firm. Place vanilla scoops in center of brownie crust; alternate scoops of chocolate and strawberry around edge. Cover and freeze until firm.

Just before serving, remove sides of pan. Arrange bananas and strawberries over ice cream. Drizzle with hot fudge and strawberry toppings. Sprinkle with toffee bits. Garnish with whipped cream and almonds. Cut into wedges. **Yield:** 10 servings.

## Brownie Baked Alaska

Carol Twardzik, Spy Hill, Saskatchewan

The name Baked Alaska originated at Delmonico's Restaurant in New York City in 1876 and was created in honor of the newly acquired territory of Alaska. This version combines a brownie base with ice cream and a meringue topping.

- 2 squares (1 ounce *each*) unsweetened chocolate
- 1/2 cup shortening
- 1 cup sugar
- 1 teaspoon vanilla extract
- 2 eggs
- 3/4 cup all-purpose flour
- 1/2 teaspoon baking powder
- 1/2 teaspoon salt
- 1 cup chopped walnuts, optional
- 1 quart strawberry ice cream, slightly softened
- 1 quart vanilla ice cream, slightly softened

MERINGUE:
- 5 egg whites
- 2/3 cup sugar
- 1/2 teaspoon cream of tartar

brownie baked alaska

In a large saucepan, melt chocolate and shortening; remove from the heat. Stir in sugar and vanilla. Add eggs, one at a time, beating well after each addition. Combine the flour, baking powder and salt; stir into chocolate mixture. Add nuts if desired.

Spread into a greased 9-in. round baking pan. Bake at 350° for 20-25 minutes or until a toothpick inserted near the center comes out with moist crumbs (do not overbake). Cool for 10 minutes before removing from pan to a wire rack to cool completely.

Meanwhile, line an 8-in. or 9-in. round bowl (1-1/2-qts.) with foil. Quickly spread strawberry ice cream over bottom and up sides of bowl, leaving center hollow; cover and freeze for 30 minutes. Pack vanilla ice cream into center; cover and freeze.

To assemble, place the brownie base on a 10-in. ovenproof serving plate. Unmold ice cream onto brownie. Return to freezer while preparing meringue.

In a heavy saucepan or double boiler over simmering water, combine the egg whites, sugar and cream of tartar. Heat over low heat while beating egg white mixture with a portable mixer on low speed for 1 minute, scraping down sides of bowl. Continue beating until mixture reaches 160°. Remove from the heat. Beat on high speed until stiff peaks form.

Quickly spread over ice cream and brownie. Bake at 500° for 2-5 minutes or until the meringue is lightly browned. (Or return to freezer until ready to bake.) Transfer to a serving plate; serve immediately. **Yield:** 12 servings.

## Chewy Brownie Cookies

Jonie Adams, Albion, Michigan

Bite into one of these chocolaty cookies and you'll discover that they offer a chewy brownie interior. Perfect for after-school snacking and lunch box treats. This is one recipe I know you'll reach for time and again. Enjoy them with coffee or glasses of cold milk.

- 2/3 cup shortening
- 1-1/2 cups packed brown sugar
- 1 tablespoon water
- 1 tablespoon vanilla extract
- 2 eggs
- 1-1/2 cups all-purpose flour
- 1/3 cup baking cocoa
- 1/2 teaspoon salt
- 1/4 teaspoon baking soda
- 2 cups (12 ounces) semisweet chocolate chips
- 1/2 cup chopped walnuts *or* pecans, optional

In a large mixing bowl, cream shortening, sugar, water and vanilla until light and fluffy. Beat in eggs. Combine flour, cocoa, salt and baking soda; gradually add to creamed mixture and beat just until blended. Stir in chocolate chips and nuts if desired.

Drop by rounded teaspoonfuls 2 in. apart on ungreased baking sheets. Bake at 375° for 7-9 minutes; do not overbake. Cool 2 minutes before removing to wire racks to cool. **Yield:** 3 dozen.

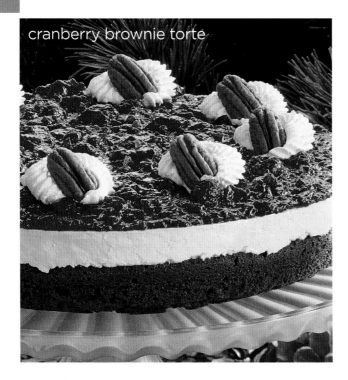

cranberry brownie torte

## Cranberry Brownie Torte

Gloria Kirchman, Eden Prairie, Minnesota

Canned cranberry sauce adds a festive finishing touch to this exquisite dessert. Folks are sure to find it irresistible, particularly during the holidays.

- 1 package fudge brownie mix (13-inch x 9-inch pan size)
- 2 eggs
- 1/2 cup vegetable oil
- 1/4 cup water
- 1/2 cup chopped pecans

FILLING:
- 1 package (8 ounces) cream cheese, softened
- 1/2 cup cranberry juice
- 2 tablespoons sugar
- 1 carton (12 ounces) frozen whipped topping, thawed

TOPPING:
- 1 can (16 ounces) whole-berry cranberry sauce

Pecan halves, optional

In a large bowl, combine the brownie mix, eggs, oil and water. Fold in pecans.

Transfer to a greased 10-in. springform pan. Bake at 350° for 35-40 minutes or until a toothpick inserted near the center comes out with moist crumbs. Cool completely on a wire rack.

For filling, in a large mixing bowl, beat the cream cheese, cranberry juice and sugar until smooth; set aside 1 cup whipped topping for garnish. Fold remaining topping into cream cheese mixture.

Carefully spread over brownie. Stir cranberry sauce; carefully spread over the filling. Garnish with reserved whipped topping and pecan halves if desired. Cover and refrigerate for at least 2 hours before serving. Refrigerate leftovers. **Yield:** 12 servings.

## Crunchy Dessert Bars

Shirley Reed, San Angelo, Texas

My son-in-law is diabetic and loves these five-ingredient, frozen dessert bars. With their nutty crunch from Grape Nuts cereal, we think they taste like a Snickers candy bar...with far less sugar.

- 1 pint fat-free no-sugar-added vanilla ice cream, softened
- 1 cup reduced-fat whipped topping
- 1/2 cup reduced-fat peanut butter
- 1 package (1.0 ounce) sugar-free instant butterscotch pudding mix
- 1 cup Grape-Nuts

In a large mixing bowl, beat the first four ingredients until smooth. Stir in cereal.

Transfer to a foil-lined 8-in. square pan. Cover and freeze for 3-4 hours or until firm. Use foil to lift out of pan; discard foil. Cut into bars. **Yield:** 2 dozen.

## Brownie Tarts

Sharon Wilkins, Grande Pointe, Ontario

I often take these from-scratch, bite-size chocolate goodies to potluck dinners for our country dance club.

- 1/2 cup butter, softened
- 1 package (3 ounces) cream cheese, softened
- 1 cup all-purpose flour

FILLING:
- 1/2 cup semisweet chocolate chips
- 2 tablespoons butter
- 1/2 cup sugar
- 1 egg, beaten
- 1 teaspoon vanilla extract
- 1/2 cup chopped pecans, optional

Maraschino cherry halves, optional

brownie tarts

toffee brownie trifle

In a large mixing bowl, cream butter and cream cheese until light and fluffy. Gradually add flour until well blended. Cover and refrigerate for 1 hour.

Shape into 1-in. balls. Place in ungreased miniature muffin cups; press into the bottom and up the sides to form a shell.

For filling, in a microwave, melt chocolate chips and butter; stir until smooth. Stir in the sugar, egg and vanilla. Add the pecans if desired. Spoon into shells.

Bake at 325° for 30-35 minutes or until a toothpick inserted near the center comes out clean. Cool 10 minutes before removing to a wire rack to cool completely. Garnish with cherries if desired. **Yield:** 2 dozen.

## Toffee Brownie Trifle

Wendy Bennett, Sioux Falls, South Dakota

This decadent combination of pantry items is a terrific way to dress up a brownie mix. Try it with other flavors of pudding or substitute your favorite candy bar. It tastes great with low-fat and sugar-free products, too.

- 1 package fudge brownie mix (13-inch x 9-inch pan size)
- 2-1/2 cups cold milk
- 1 package (3.4 ounces) instant cheesecake *or* vanilla pudding mix
- 1 package (3.3 ounces) instant white chocolate pudding mix
- 1 carton (8 ounces) frozen whipped topping, thawed
- 2 to 3 Heath candy bars (1.4 ounces *each*), chopped

Prepare and bake brownies according to package directions for cake-like brownies, using a greased 13-in. x 9-in. x 2-in. baking pan. Cool completely on a wire rack.

In a large mixing bowl, beat the milk and pudding mixes on low speed for 2 minutes. Fold in whipped topping. Cut the brownies into 1-in. cubes; place half in a 3-qt. glass trifle bowl or serving dish. Cover with half of the pudding. Repeat layers. Sprinkle with chopped candy bars. Refrigerate leftovers. **Yield:** 16 servings.

## Hugs 'n' Kisses Brownie

Kristi Van Batavia, Kansas City, Missouri

When I needed a dessert in a hurry, I dressed up a boxed mix with on-hand ingredients to come up with this impressive brownie treat.

- 1 package fudge brownie mix (8-inch square pan size)
- 1 egg
- 1/4 cup vegetable oil
- 1/4 cup water
- 1-1/2 cups vanilla *or* white chips, *divided*
- 14 to 16 milk chocolate kisses
- 14 to 16 striped chocolate kisses
- 1-1/2 teaspoons shortening

In a large bowl, stir brownie mix, egg, oil and water until well blended. Fold in 1 cup vanilla chips.

Pour into a greased 9-in. heart-shaped or round springform pan. Bake at 350° for 35-40 minutes or until a toothpick inserted 2-in. from the side of pan comes out clean.

Let stand for 10 minutes; alternate milk chocolate and striped kisses around edge of pan with points toward center. Melt shortening and remaining chips; stir until smooth. Drizzle over brownie. Cool completely. Remove sides of springform pan. **Yield:** 10-12 servings.

hugs 'n' kisses brownie

## Decadent Brownie Pie

Stephanie Vozzo, Belvidere, New Jersey

You'll love this favorite of mine. It is the richest brownie you'll ever taste. You can dress it up with different garnishes if you like, but the thick chocolate ganache is always a hit on its own.

|       |                              |
|-------|------------------------------|
| 2/3   | cup butter, softened         |
| 1-1/4 | cups sugar                   |
| 1/2   | cup light corn syrup         |
| 2     | eggs                         |
| 1-1/4 | cups all-purpose flour       |
| 1/2   | cup baking cocoa             |
| 1/2   | teaspoon salt                |
| 3     | tablespoons milk             |
| 2     | cups chopped walnuts         |

GANACHE:

|   |                                        |
|---|----------------------------------------|
| 1 | cup heavy whipping cream               |
| 8 | squares (1 ounce *each*) semisweet chocolate, chopped |

Mint Andes candies, fresh raspberries, fresh mint leaves, caramel ice cream topping and whipped cream, optional

In a large mixing bowl, cream butter and sugar until light and fluffy. Beat in corn syrup. Add eggs, one at a time, beating well after each addition. Combine the flour, cocoa and salt; gradually add to creamed mixture alternately with milk. Fold in walnuts.

Spread into a greased 10-in. springform pan. Bake at 325° for 55-60 minutes or until a toothpick inserted 1 in. from the side of pan comes out clean. Cool on a wire rack.

For ganache, in a small saucepan, bring cream to a boil. Remove from the heat; stir in chocolate until melted. Cool completely. Remove sides of springform pan. Place a wire rack over waxed paper; set brownie on rack.

Pour ganache over the brownie; spread over top and let drip down sides. Let stand until set. Cut into wedges; garnish with desired toppings. Store in the refrigerator. **Yield:** 10-12 servings.

brownie delight

## Brownie Delight

Opal Erickson, Branson, Missouri

Brownie mix and instant pudding hurry along the preparation of this scrumptious layered dessert. My family even asks for this treat for their birthdays instead of cake.

|     |                                                                |
|-----|----------------------------------------------------------------|
| 1   | package brownie mix (13-inch x 9-inch pan size)                |
| 2   | packages (one 8 ounces, one 3 ounces) cream cheese, softened   |
| 2   | cups confectioners' sugar                                      |
| 1   | carton (16 ounces) frozen whipped topping, thawed, *divided*   |
| 2   | cups cold milk                                                 |
| 1   | package (3.9 ounces) instant chocolate pudding mix             |
| 1/2 | cup chopped pecans                                             |

Prepare and bake brownies according to package directions. Cool completely on a wire rack.

In a large mixing bowl, beat cream cheese and sugar until creamy. Fold in 2 cups whipped topping. Spread over brownies. In a small bowl, whisk milk and dry pudding mix for 2 minutes. Refrigerate for 5 minutes; spread over the cream cheese layer. Spread with remaining whipped topping; sprinkle with pecans. Chill until serving. **Yield:** 12-15 servings.

## Brownie Pizza

Loretta Wohlenhaus, Cumberland, Iowa

Kids of all ages will find this a delightfully different way to serve brownies. Use whatever sweet toppings to suit your family's tastes.

|       |                          |
|-------|--------------------------|
| 3/4   | cup butter, softened     |
| 1     | cup sugar                |
| 1     | egg                      |
| 1     | teaspoon vanilla extract |
| 1-1/2 | cups all-purpose flour   |
| 1/4   | cup baking cocoa         |

decadent brownie pie

1/2  teaspoon baking powder
1/4  teaspoon salt
3/4  cup milk chocolate M&M's, *divided*
1/2  cup chopped walnuts, *divided*
1/4  cup miniature marshmallows
1/4  cup flaked coconut

In a large mixing bowl, cream butter and sugar until light and fluffy. Beat in egg and vanilla. Combine the flour, cocoa, baking powder and salt; gradually add to creamed mixture until well blended. Stir in 1/2 cup M&M's and 1/4 cup walnuts.

Spread onto a greased 14-in. pizza pan to within 1/2 in. of edges. Sprinkle with remaining M&M's and walnuts. Top with marshmallows and coconut. Bake at 350° for 15-20 minutes or until a toothpick inserted near the center comes out clean. Cool on a wire rack. Cut into wedges. **Yield:** 10-12 servings.

## Mint Brownie Cupcakes

Carol Maertz, Spruce Grove, Alberta

Are they a brownie or are they a cupcake? There's no wrong answer to this question, I tell my first-grade students. I found the recipe when I began teaching nearly 20 years ago. I still love to bake these sweet surprises for my husband and our children. They're great for kids' parties and coffee get-togethers with friends.

1    cup mint chocolate chips
1/2  cup butter
1/2  cup sugar
2    eggs
1/2  cup all-purpose flour
1    teaspoon baking powder
TOPPING:
4    cups miniature marshmallows
3/4  cup milk
1-1/2 teaspoons peppermint extract

mint brownie cupcakes

Green *or* red food coloring, optional
1-1/2  cups heavy whipping cream, whipped
Additional chocolate chips, optional

In a heavy saucepan, melt chips and butter; stir until smooth. Remove from the heat.

Stir in sugar and eggs. Combine flour and baking powder; gradually stir into chocolate mixture until smooth.

Fill paper-lined muffin cups half full. Bake at 350° for 15-20 minutes or until a toothpick comes out clean (cupcakes will fall in center). Remove from pan to a wire rack to cool.

In a large saucepan, cook and stir marshmallows and milk over low heat until smooth. Remove from the heat; stir in extract and food coloring if desired.

Cover and refrigerate for about 15 minutes or until cool. Fold in whipped cream. Spread over cupcakes or top each with a dollop of topping. Refrigerate for at least 1 hour. Sprinkle with chocolate chips if desired. Store in the refrigerator. **Yield:** 16 cupcakes.

brownie pizza

## Brownie Point

To keep frosted brownies, cupcakes and other desserts from sticking to aluminum foil when covering them, consider this idea. Mold a sheet of aluminum foil over an upturned bowl that's a little larger than the plate. Remove the domed foil, place it over the serving plate and tuck in the edges.

# General Recipe Index

Mint Brownie Cupcakes, 107
Mint Brownie Pie, 101
Mocha Brownies, 27
Mocha Mousse Brownies, 70
Mocha Truffle Brownies, 6
Moist Cake Brownies, 18
Napoleon Cremes, 76
No-Bake Peanut Brownies, 57
No-Fuss Fudgy Brownies, 98
Peanut Butter Brownies, 62
Peanutty Caramel Bars, 86
Peppermint Oat Bars, 90
Raspberry Brownies a la Mode, 48
Raspberry Truffle Brownies, 74
Rocky Road Brownies, 58
Saucepan Brownies, 90
Simply Fudgy Brownies, 23
Sweet Chocolate Bars, 24
Triple-Chocolate Brownie Squares, 22
Two-Tone Fudge Brownies, 9
Witch Hat Treats, 73
Zebra Sweets, 72

### CHOCOLATE SYRUP & TOPPING
Banana Split Brownie Pie, 102
Berries 'n Cream Brownies, 38
Chocolate Bliss Brownies, 33
Creamy Cashew Brownies, 78
Triple-Chocolate Brownie Squares, 22

### COCONUT
Almond Coconut Brownies, 66
Almond Macaroon Brownies, 67
Apricot-Coconut Bars, 44
Black 'n' White Brownies, 75
Brownie Caramel Parfaits, 100
Brownie Pizza, 106
Chewy Granola Bars, 87
Chewy Peanut Butter Bars, 67
Chocolate Chip Brownies, 26
Chocolate Maple Bars, 30
Coconut Chip Nut Bars, 63
Coconut Cranberry Bars, 43
Coconut Granola Bars, 60
Coconut Raspberry Bars, 39
Diamond Bars, 92
Dream Bars, 63
Fruit Cocktail Bars, 45
German Chocolate Cheesecake Bars, 25
Layered Coconut Bars, 39
Lime Coconut Bars, 36
Macaroon Brownies, 12
Merry Cherry Bars, 48
Napoleon Cremes, 76
Peanut Butter Squares, 10
Pineapple Coconut Squares, 45
Rhubarb Dream Bars, 42
Strawberry Oatmeal Bars, 50
Sweet Chocolate Bars, 24
Toffee Nut Squares, 56
Walnut Cookie Strips, 55

### COFFEE
Cappuccino Cake Brownies, 14
Cinnamon Brownies, 85
Mocha Brownies, 27
Mocha Mousse Brownie Trifle, 99
Mocha Mousse Brownies, 70
Mocha Truffle Brownies, 6
Raisin Cinnamon Bars, 47
Raspberry Truffle Brownies, 74
Rich Chocolate Brownies, 31
Treasured Brownies, 11

### CRANBERRIES
Coconut Cranberry Bars, 43
Cranberry Brownie Torte, 104
Cranberry-Orange Bars, 38
Cranberry Popcorn Bars, 92
Cranberry Walnut Bars, 63
Crimson Crumble Bars, 49
Frosted Pumpkin Cranberry Bars, 13

### CREAM CHEESE
Almond Macaroon Brownies, 67
Banana-Berry Brownie Pizza, 42
Black 'n' White Brownies, 75
Brownie Cheesecake, 98
Brownie Delight, 106
Brownie Tarts, 104
Butterscotch Bars, 67
Cheesecake Brownies, 100
Cheesecake Squares, 14
Chocolate Cheese Layered Bars, 10
Chocolate Cheesecake Squares, 26
Chocolate Chip Cheesecake Bars, 17
Chocolate Lemon Cream Bars, 40
Chocolate Raspberry Bars, 76
Cranberry Brownie Torte, 104
Cream Cheese Swirl Brownies, 8
Creamy Cashew Brownies, 78
Fruit 'n Nut Spice Bars, 50
Fruity Brownie Pizza, 49
Fudgy Mint Squares, 9
German Chocolate Cheesecake Bars, 25
Layered Brownie Dessert, 96
Lemon Cheesecake Squares, 40
Marble Brownies, 30
Marble Chocolate Cheesecake Bars, 28
Marbled Chocolate Bars, 23
Mint Brownie Pie, 101
Mocha Mousse Brownies, 70
Mocha Truffle Brownies, 6
Peaches 'n Cream Bars, 42
Peanut Butter Brownies, 62
Peanut Butter Squares, 10
Pear Custard Bars, 15
Pecan Cream Cheese Squares, 65
Peppermint Oat Bars, 90
Raspberry Truffle Brownies, 74
Rich Cheesecake Bars, 90
Teddy Carrot Bars, 74

### FRUIT (also see specific kinds)
Fruit Cocktail Bars, 45
Fruitcake Squares, 44

### GERMAN SWEET CHOCOLATE
Banana Split Brownie Pie, 102
Toffee Squares, 84

### GRAHAM CRACKERS
Coconut Cranberry Bars, 43
Double Chip Bars, 93
Gooey Chip Bars, 54
Layered Brownie Cookies, 93
Lemon Graham Squares, 39
Napoleon Cremes, 76
No-Bake Peanut Brownies, 57

### HAZELNUTS
Fudgy Nut Brownies, 79
Hazelnut Brownies, 65
Rustic Nut Bars, 60

### HONEY
Granola Fruit Bars, 41
Honey Pecan Triangles, 16

Peanut Butter-Honey Bars, 86
Rustic Nut Bars, 60
Sunflower Popcorn Bars, 91

### ICE CREAM
Banana Split Brownie Pie, 102
Brownie Baked Alaska, 103
Brownie Caramel Parfaits, 100
Brownie Pie a la Mode, 102
Crunchy Dessert Bars, 104
Giant Ice Cream Sandwich, 100
Strawberry Brownie Bombe, 97

### LEMON & LIME
Chocolate Lemon Cream Bars, 40
Classic Lemon Bars, 87
Lemon Cheesecake Squares, 40
Lemon Graham Squares, 39
Lime Coconut Bars, 36
Lime Cooler Bars, 51
Macadamia Lemon Bars, 84
Raspberry Citrus Bars, 41

### M&M'S
Brownie Pizza, 106
Candy Cereal Treats, 84
Fudge-Filled Bars, 24
Fun Marshmallow Bars, 89
Golden M&M Bars, 62
M&M Oat Bars, 88

### MACADAMIA NUTS
Caramel Macadamia Nut Brownies, 61
Macadamia Chip Brownies, 56
Macadamia Lemon Bars, 84
Pear Custard Bars, 15
Snow Flurry Brownies, 7

### MARSHMALLOWS & MARSHMALLOW CREME
Almond Coconut Brownies, 66
Brownie Pizza, 106
Candy Cereal Treats, 84
Caramel Corn Chocolate Bars, 54
Chewy Granola Bars, 87
Chocolate Cheese Layered Bars, 10
Chocolate Crunch Brownies, 19
Chocolate Maple Bars, 30
Chocolate Peanut Butter Treats, 85
Cranberry Popcorn Bars, 92
Frosted Cookie Brownies, 77
Fun Marshmallow Bars, 89
Heavenly Hash Bars, 62
Macaroon Brownies, 12
Marshmallow Brownies, 29
Mint Brownie Cupcakes, 107
No-Bake Raisin Bars, 86
Peanut Mallow Bars, 55
Really Rocky Road Brownies, 24
Rocky Road Brownies, 58
Salted Nut Squares, 66
Witch Hat Treats, 73
Zebra Sweets, 72

### MINT
Fudgy Mint Squares, 9
Glazed Mint Brownies, 79
Mint Brownie Cupcakes, 107
Mint Brownie Pie, 101
Peppermint Oat Bars, 90
Peppermint Patty Brownies, 58

### MOLASSES
Spice Bars, 91
Spice Cake Bars, 75

**NUTS** (also see Almonds; Cashews; Hazelnuts; Macadamia Nuts; Peanuts; Pecans; Pistachios; Walnuts)
Cheesecake Brownies, 100
Chocolate Bliss Brownies, 33
Chocolate Date Squares, 46
Cranberry-Orange Bars, 38
Favorite Cake Brownies, 32
Gift-Wrapped Brownies, 80
Glazed Persimmon Bars, 46
Heavenly Hash Bars, 62
Jewel Nut Bars, 11
Layered Brownies, 25
Merry Cherry Bars, 48
Nutty Brownies, 88
Toffee Nut Squares, 56
Toffee Squares, 84
Treasured Brownies, 11

**OATS**
Apricot Oat Bars, 37
Banana Cocoa Brownies, 50
Black 'n' White Brownies, 75
Blueberry Oat Bars, 40
Butterscotch Bars, 67
Caramel-Chocolate Oat Squares, 12
Chewy Granola Bars, 87
Chocolate Caramel Bars, 64
Chocolate Chip Oat Bars, 65
Chocolate Oatmeal Bars, 25
Coconut Granola Bars, 60
Crimson Crumble Bars, 49
Date Bar Dessert, 37
Frosted Peanut Butter Fingers, 17
Fudge-Filled Bars, 24
Granola Fruit Bars, 41
Lemon Cheesecake Squares, 40
M&M Oat Bars, 88
Microwave Oatmeal Bars, 75
Peanut Jelly Bars, 47
Peanut Mallow Bars, 55
Peppermint Oat Bars, 90
Sour Cream Raisin Squares, 14
Spiced Apple Bars, 51
Strawberry Oatmeal Bars, 50

**ORANGE**
Cranberry-Orange Bars, 38
Orange Slice Bars, 58
Raspberry Citrus Bars, 41

**PACKAGED BROWNIE MIX**
Banana-Berry Brownie Pizza, 42
Banana Cream Brownie Dessert, 19
Berries 'n Cream Brownies, 38
Brownie Caramel Parfaits, 100
Brownie Delight, 106
Caramel Brownie Pizza, 56
Chocolate Chip Brownies, 26
Cranberry Brownie Torte, 104
Creamy Cashew Brownies, 78
Double Frosted Brownies, 76
Football Brownies, 72
Frosted Cake Brownies, 71
Fruity Brownie Pizza, 49
Giant Ice Cream Sandwich, 100
Hugs 'n' Kisses Brownie, 105
Mini Brownie Treats, 97
Mocha Brownies, 27
Peanut Butter Brownie Cups, 89
Strawberry Brownie Bombe, 97
Toffee Brownie Trifle, 105
Triple-Chocolate Brownie Squares, 22
Valentine Brownies, 80

**PACKAGED CAKE MIX**
Cheesecake Brownies, 100
Chocolate Chip Cake Bars, 86
Chocolate Lemon Cream Bars, 40
Chocolate Raspberry Bars, 76
Fun Marshmallow Bars, 89
German Chocolate Bars, 22
Layered Brownies, 25
Marbled Chocolate Bars, 23
Peanut Butter Caramel Bars, 54
Pecan Cream Cheese Squares, 65
Quick Brownies, 89
Rich Cheesecake Bars, 90

**PACKAGED COOKIES**
Brownie Cheesecake, 98
Double Chocolate Bars, 31
Fruitcake Squares, 44
Layered Coconut Bars, 39
Lime Coconut Bars, 36

**PACKAGED PUDDING & MOUSSE MIX**
Banana Cream Brownie Dessert, 19
Brownie Delight, 106
Crunchy Dessert Bars, 104
Double Frosted Brownies, 76
Layered Brownie Dessert, 96
Mocha Mousse Brownie Trifle, 99
Napoleon Cremes, 76
Toffee Brownie Trifle, 105
Triple-Chocolate Brownie Squares, 22

**PEACHES**
Peaches 'n Cream Bars, 42

**PEANUT BUTTER**
Banana Crunch Bars, 93
Candy Cereal Treats, 84
Chewy Granola Bars, 87
Chewy Peanut Butter Bars, 67
Chocolate Crunch Brownies, 19
Chocolate Oatmeal Bars, 25
Chocolate Peanut Butter Treats, 85
Coconut Granola Bars, 60
Crunchy Dessert Bars, 104
Double Chip Bars, 93
Frosted Peanut Butter Fingers, 17
Granola Fruit Bars, 41
Heavenly Hash Bars, 62
No-Bake Peanut Brownies, 57
Peanut Butter Brownie Cups, 89
Peanut Butter Brownies, 62
Peanut Butter Caramel Bars, 54
Peanut Butter-Honey Bars, 86
Peanut Butter Squares, 10
Peanutty Caramel Bars, 86
Quick Brownies, 89
Sunflower Popcorn Bars, 91
Witch Hat Treats, 73

**PEANUTS**
Banana Cream Brownie Dessert, 19
Candy Cereal Treats, 84
Chewy Granola Bars, 87
Fun Marshmallow Bars, 89
No-Bake Peanut Brownies, 57
Peanut Butter Caramel Bars, 54
Peanut Butter Squares, 10
Peanut Cookie Bars, 88
Peanut Jelly Bars, 47
Peanut Mallow Bars, 55
Peanutty Caramel Bars, 86
Salted Nut Squares, 66

**PEARS**
Pear Custard Bars, 15

**PECANS**
Brownie Caramel Parfaits, 100
Brownie Cheesecake, 98
Brownie Cups, 32
Brownie Delight, 106
Brownie Tarts, 104
Butter Fudge Fingers, 6
Butterscotch Bars, 67
Caramel Brownie Pizza, 56
Caramel Corn Chocolate Bars, 54
Cherry Streusel Squares, 48
Chippy Blond Brownies, 60
Choco-Cloud Brownies, 71
Chocolate Caramel Bars, 64
Chocolate Cheese Layered Bars, 10
Chocolate Chip Brownies, 26
Chocolate Chip Cake Bars, 86
Chocolate Chip Cheesecake Bars, 17
Chocolate Chip Oat Bars, 65
Chocolate Maple Bars, 30
Chocolate Toffee Crunchies, 32
Coconut Cranberry Bars, 43
Cranberry Brownie Torte, 104
Crimson Crumble Bars, 49
Cupcake Brownies, 101
Fruitcake Squares, 44
Fruity Brownie Pizza, 49
Fudge-Filled Bars, 24
German Chocolate Cheesecake Bars, 25
Granola Fruit Bars, 41
Honey Pecan Triangles, 16
Moist Cake Brownies, 18
No-Fuss Fudgy Brownies, 98
Pecan Cream Cheese Squares, 65
Pecan Pie Bars, 57
Pecan-Toffee Bars, 59
Raisin Cinnamon Bars, 47
Raspberry Nut Bars, 36
Sweet Chocolate Bars, 24
Toffee Bars, 28
Triple-Nut Diamonds, 59

**PERSIMMONS**
Glazed Persimmon Bars, 46

**PINEAPPLE**
Crimson Crumble Bars, 49
Fruitcake Squares, 44
Fruity Brownie Pizza, 49
Pineapple Coconut Squares, 45

**PISTACHIOS**
Rustic Nut Bars, 60

**POPCORN**
Caramel Corn Chocolate Bars, 54
Cranberry Popcorn Bars, 92
Sunflower Popcorn Bars, 91

**PREPARED BROWNIES**
Brownie Cheesecake, 98
Mocha Mousse Brownie Trifle, 99

**PUMPKIN**
Frosted Pumpkin Cranberry Bars, 13

**RAISINS & DATES**
Chewy Granola Bars, 87
Chocolate Date Squares, 46
Date Bar Dessert, 37
Fruitcake Squares, 44

# Alphabetical Index